Teach® Yourself

Successful Budgeting and Forecasting

Roger Mason

www.inaweek.co.uk

IN A WEEK

Hodder Education

338 Euston Road, London NW1 3BH.

Hodder Education is an Hachette UK company

First published in UK 2013 by Hodder Education

This edition published 2013

Copyright © 2013 Roger Mason

The moral rights of the author have been asserted

Database right Hodder Education (makers)

British Library Cataloguing in Publication Data: a catalogue record for this title is
available from the British Library.

10 9 8 7 6 5 4 3 2 1

The publisher has used its best endeavours to ensure that any website
addresses referred to in this book are correct and active at the time of going
to press. However, the publisher and the author have no responsibility for the
websites and can make no guarantee that a site will remain live or that the
content will remain relevant, decent or appropriate.

The publisher has made every effort to mark as such all words which it
believes to be trademarks. The publisher should also like to make it clear that
the presence of a word in the book, whether marked or unmarked, in no way
affects its legal status as a trademark.

Every reasonable effort has been made by the publisher to trace the copyright
holders of material in this book. Any errors or omissions should be notified
in writing to the publisher, who will endeavour to rectify the situation for any
reprints and future editions.

Hachette UK's policy is to use papers that are natural, renewable and
recyclable products and made from wood grown in sustainable forests.
The logging and manufacturing processes are expected to conform to the
environmental regulations of the country of origin.

www.hoddereducation.co.uk

Typeset by Cenveo Publisher Services.

Printed in Great Britain by CPI Group (UK) Ltd, Croydon, CR0 4YY

Also available
in ebook

Contents

Introduction

The precise number depends on the definition used, but there are well over 1 million managers in Britain and countless others around the world. In both the public sector and the private sector many of them are involved in budgeting and forecasting. It is probably true to say that a significant number of them – by no means all, of course – do not particularly enjoy this aspect of their job, resent the time commitment and sometimes doubt the value of the end product. This is a shame because budgets and forecasts are important, to their companies or other employers and to them personally.

A mastery of budgeting and forecasting will help managers do their job more effectively and it will help with their career development too. It is important at any time, but especially so in times of recession and economic difficulty. The section at the back of the book about surviving in tough times may be particularly important and should not be neglected.

This book should help managers understand the basic principles and it should help many of them progress further. This has to be good news – for their employers and for them too. They will then be more likely to value their work and the resulting budgets and forecasts, and they might even enjoy doing them.

Budgets and forecasts are often prepared with reference to a pyramid structure. Many managers are responsible for just one cost centre or department and their budgets are likely to be expenditure budgets. Other managers, probably more senior ones, are responsible for a number of these cost centres or departments and perhaps for revenue budgets as well. Senior managers are responsible for the total budgets and forecasts. If they are wise, the senior managers will try to involve their more junior colleagues as much as possible. This book takes account of the fact that budgets are often organized in this way.

This introduction is a good place to confess that in writing the book I have had some difficulties with the terms 'budget' and 'forecast'. The difference between them is explained at the beginning of the first chapter, but in many instances they can be used interchangeably. Rather than litter the book with extraneous words I have used just the word 'budget' in many places. You can nearly always take it that this includes a forecast.

The book contains 70 end-of-chapter questions, each with four possible answers. The correct answers are given at the end of the book. I do hope that you attempt them. If you get 60 correct, that is a good score – anything higher is exceptional.

I have enjoyed writing this book and I hope that you enjoy reading it, or at the very least find it useful. My best wishes for your future success.

Roger Mason

SUNDAY

Budgeting and forecasting fundamentals

It is a sound military principle that time spent reconnoitring is not wasted. From Tuesday through to Friday we will be examining and reviewing the different budgets and forecasts and how they are prepared. On Saturday we will look at how the budgets and forecasts should be used after they have been approved. However, we start the week by reconnoitring the subject, establishing some important principles and answering some key questions.

The topics covered comprise:

- The differences between plans, forecasts and budgets
- Are budgets and forecasts important?
- The value and purposes of budgets and forecasts
- Should budgets and forecasts be left to the accountants?
- Should budgets and forecasts be only for large organizations?
- The right period for budgets and forecasts
- Are budgets and forecasts only relevant for an organization that has an income?
- Should budgets and forecasts be optimistic or realistic?
- Top-down or bottom-up?
- Budget assumptions
- Limiting factors
- Seasonal factors

The differences between plans, forecasts and budgets

The three terms are often confused and used in an interchangeable way. This is understandable but wrong. They are different and the differences should be understood.

Plan

This is a set of approved policies and targets for the future, and they need not be expressed in financial terms. For example, there may be a plan to achieve a position where 50 per cent of a country's population recognize a company's name. Of course, plans normally have financial implications. If only 30 per cent of a country's population currently recognize a company's name and it is intended that in three years' time this should increase to 50 per cent, it is probable that money must be spent. This expenditure will in the short term reduce both profits and cash, though in time the increased expenditure will, presumably and hopefully, have the opposite effect and increase sales (and therefore profits) and also cash.

Forecast

This is a prediction of what will happen and it is often expressed in financial terms. A forecast differs from a budget in that it is not a target. Forecasts are usually prepared and laid out in the same way as budgets, but the difference is a belief that they state what will actually happen. A budget, on the other hand, is a target and represents an aim that it is hoped (with greater or lesser confidence) will be achieved. Of course, a realistic budget is close to being a forecast.

Budget

This is a plan expressed in financial terms. There may be a single budget, which will probably be a profit budget, or a series of linked budgets. This is desirable because the linked budgets will all be useful and because they will each contribute to the realism and value of the others. For example a financial change in any budget must have an effect on the budgeted balance sheet. A budget is a target rather than a forecast and subsequent results can be monitored against it. This is to see if the budget is being achieved and, if it is not, exactly what has gone wrong and where remedial action needs to be taken. Whether budget targets should be achievable easily or only with great effort is examined later today.

Are budgets and forecasts important?

Not everyone thinks that businesses should bother with budgets and forecasts, and not all businesses have them. Some managers dislike preparing them and resent their performance being monitored against them afterwards. Furthermore, they may take up a considerable amount of managers' time and, as we all know, managers' time is valuable and often in short supply. Nevertheless, budgets and forecasts are important, and if well done should be worth the time and effort put into them. The value and purposes of budgets and forecasts are reviewed next, but for now consider your answers to the following seven questions. If the answer to any of them is no, you should see why budgets and forecasts are important.

1 Do you know if the business is going to run out of cash?
2 Is your business going to make a satisfactory profit in the next year?
3 Is your company at risk of going out of business and, if so, what needs to be done to stop it happening?
4 Is your business making the maximum possible profit?
5 Is there any waste that could be cut out?
6 Do you know which departments and sections are performing efficiently and which ones are not?
7 Have you got the information to make improvements in the way that your business is run?

The value and purposes of budgets and forecasts

Budgets and forecasts enable, or perhaps force, managers to plan ahead logically and constructively, and they enable, or perhaps force, top managers to study how different parts of the business interact. They enable managers to anticipate any limiting factors and plan how they can be overcome. For example, a business may be steadily expanding in a profitable and satisfactory manner, but budgeting may reveal an impending shortage of working capital or storage facilities.

'Give us the tools and we will finish the job.' This unforgettable phrase was addressed to President Roosevelt by the Prime Minister, Winston Churchill, in a broadcast on 9 February 1941. In a completely different context it could well be adopted for budgets and forecasts. Information can be a vital tool for both senior and junior managers. Using it well should help them finish the job, which is to operate effectively and plan ahead to achieve the best possible results.

In the unlikely event that nothing whatsoever is done with the completed budgets, the discipline of preparing them has still forced managers to plan the future logically. This means considering such things as:

- Where do we intend to be at the end of the budget period?
- How a department and budget interacts with other departments and other budgets.
- Are there any limiting factors and what are they?
- Should we be aware of any particular dangers and, if so, what should be done about them?
- What actions must be taken to achieve the budgeted results?
- What are realistic, achievable targets to set ourselves?

Of course, it is highly desirable that the budgets are afterwards used as a control tool and most organizations do use them in this way. Regular reports should enable managers to see departures from the budgeted figures and take correcting action. This is covered in detail on Saturday.

Should budgets and forecasts be left to the accountants?

Most thoughtful people answer 'no' to this question; this is also my strong opinion, and I am an accountant. Nevertheless, there are arguments that can be made for making budgets and forecasts the responsibility of only the accountants. They include:

- The job will probably be done more quickly.
- There will be no encroachment on the valuable time of the other managers, who will be left free to do whatever it is that they do. For example, sales managers will spend more time selling and production managers will spend more time producing.
- Many non-financial managers do not like working on budgets and forecasts and, strange as it might seem, many financial managers do enjoy it. Perhaps the best results may be obtained from people who enjoy what they are doing.

The probably more compelling arguments for involving the non-financial managers include:

- The resulting budget or forecast is more likely to be realistic. The non-financial managers may well have information not known to the accountants, and they will probably have a good idea about what can and cannot be achieved.
- The non-financial managers will hopefully be able to suggest sensible changes and efficiency savings.
- The budget or forecast is likely to be better and, which is extremely important, it is much more likely that all managers will feel committed to it afterwards. If they have contributed to it, they should feel a sense of ownership. Of course the budget may not be exactly what they want but it might be, and at the very least they should feel that their points of view have had a fair hearing and been taken into account.

Whether or not non-financial managers have contributed, it is almost certainly best that the accountants should co-ordinate the budgets and forecasts. They are best placed to see that the final budgets are complete and without inconsistencies. Regardless of how they are prepared and reviewed, final approval should be given at a very high level.

Budgets and forecasts is a rather serious subject, so perhaps a little humour might help us concentrate. It is often said that many accountants are introverts, which helps us know if a man is an accountant. An accountant will look at his shoes rather than look you in the eye. The only people more introverted than accountants are actuaries. An actuary will look at his own shoes rather than your shoes.

Should budgets and forecasts only be for large organizations?

The answer to this question is no. Small organizations and even one-person businesses potentially have all the issues and needs of large businesses. The figures will be smaller, but the need for good budgets and good forecasts is just as compelling.

The right period for budgets and forecasts

Budgets and forecasts most often cover a period of a year. This is because most companies prepare their statutory accounts for this length of time and many other organizations do the same. There are obvious advantages in having the budget or forecast period correspond with the financial reporting period. 'What's the profit going to be for this year?' is a frequently asked question. Having budgets and forecasts for the same period makes it easier to give an informed answer.

Having said that, there is no law or rule that makes this compulsory. Unlike most accounts, budgets and forecasts do not have to be published. You can have whatever period you like for whatever reason you like.

The divisions within a budget period of a year are often monthly, but they do not have to be. Perhaps weekly or some other period would be more appropriate. An obvious problem is that the length of a calendar month varies between 28 days and 31 days. Many budgets and forecasts are based on 13 four-week periods in order to make each period comparable with the others. This leaves just one spare day (two in a leap year) to add in somewhere. There are no rules, so do what is best in your individual circumstances.

Are budgets and forecasts only relevant for an organization that has an income?

The answer to this question is no, of course not. Organizations and departments that just spend money should strive to do so effectively and efficiently, and good expenditure budgets should be useful tools in achieving these desirable ends. Sections of central and local government come into this category. In the UK, Her Majesty's Revenue & Customs (HMRC) is an obvious example, even though it will insist on calling taxpayers its customers. As taxpayers we all wish it well in its efforts to control costs and perform efficiently.

If your direct interest is only in expenditure budgets and forecasts, parts of this book will not be immediately relevant to you. On the other hand, perhaps your next job will be managing director of a large company and with a salary to match, so perhaps you had better pay attention to the whole book.

Should budgets and forecasts be optimistic or realistic?

For forecasts the answer to this question should be self-evident. They should be neither optimistic nor pessimistic, and if they are one or the other they should not really be called forecasts. They should of course be realistic. This does not mean that they will be exactly achieved, but it does mean that at the time of preparation they represent what is considered to be the midpoint of likely outcomes. Forecasts should not necessarily be the figures first submitted. They should be these numbers adjusted to reflect changes and improvements that can confidently be predicted.

There are different opinions concerning the degree of optimism that should be incorporated into budgets. The following is a review of some of the options.

Easily achievable

Very few advocate this, though it does have the advantage that nasty surprises are unlikely. The big disadvantage is that it will provide no motivation for managers to innovate, work hard and generally strive to reach their targets. They will be able to do so in 'cruise mode' and will have no budgetary incentive to do better.

The midpoint of the likely outcomes

The difference between a budget and a forecast can be a very narrow distinction, so a realistic budget would perhaps be better called a forecast. Indeed, budgets are sometimes called budgetary forecasts. A good forecast has many virtues, but a disadvantage is that it does not set managers achievable targets beyond the middle range of likely outcomes.

Ambitious but definitely achievable

Managers are set budgetary targets that cannot easily be attained. They will have to work hard in order to do so. Nevertheless, the targets are definitely achievable. They are not so ambitious that managers will give up because they can see no prospect of success.

Extremely difficult to achieve

Managers are set budgetary targets that are so difficult that there is a high risk that they will fail to achieve them. Only with skill, exceptional effort and perhaps luck will they do so. An advantage is that it might get exceptional results from exceptional people, but a disadvantage is the high risk of failure and demotivation. If this approach is adopted, the result must clearly be regarded as a budget and not a forecast. There may be unfortunate consequences, perhaps including running out of money, if the business is over-dependent on such a budget being achieved.

Most people think that *Ambitious but definitely achievable* is the best, and this is my opinion.

Top-down or bottom-up?

There are many different approaches to budgeting but two in particular should be mentioned:

Bottom-up method

Each manager and department is required to submit budget proposals. They are given few, if any, targets and are simply encouraged to submit good proposals in the interests of the organization. When all the budget proposals have been received, they are collated into the master budgets, which may or may not be acceptable. If they are not acceptable, then top management calls for revisions.

SUNDAY

MONDAY

TUESDAY

WEDNESDAY

THURSDAY

FRIDAY

SATURDAY

Top-down method

Top management issues budget targets. Lower levels of management must then submit proposals that achieve these targets.

Each method has advantages and disadvantages. The bottom-up method may encourage managers to be innovative and realistic, and they may later feel more committed to the budgets that they have shaped. On the other hand, they may be lazy and make unrealistic submissions. When using the bottom-up method, managers will still need to be informed of limiting factors in other departments, and it may be helpful for them to be informed of significant parameters.

In practice there is often less difference between the two methods than might be supposed. It is important that at some stage there be a full and frank exchange of views. Everyone should be encouraged to put forward any constructive point of view and everyone should commit themselves to listening with an open mind. Needless to say, top management will and should have the final decisions.

Budget assumptions

Whether the adopted philosophy is top-down or bottom-up, or indeed some variation or other method, it is usually sensible for top management to issue some budget assumptions that should be used. Examples could be:

- An average 5 per cent wage increase on 1 April.
- Interest rates to be unchanged.
- Necessary funds will be provided by the parent company.
- The main government contract will be renewed on the same terms.
- No competitor will enter or leave the market.
- Rent payable will increase by 10 per cent on 1 April.
- General inflation in the economy will be 4 per cent.

Without assumptions such as these, managers may make uninformed and conflicting proposals.

Please list six sensible budget assumptions besides those above.

Limiting factors

Many budgets amount to a plan for expansion, and it is sometimes the case that one or more limiting factors must be taken into account. These may be obvious before budgeting work starts or they may become apparent while the budget is being prepared. It is important that limiting factors be recognized. It will then be necessary to incorporate into the budget some action to remove them, and this usually involves spending money. Alternatively it may be decided that, in this budget period at least, expansion will take place only up to the point of the limiting factor and not beyond.

An example of a limiting factor is a vital warehouse that is continually 85 per cent full, and at certain times of the year is 90 per cent full. This could be a limiting factor if planned expansion is more than 15 per cent and perhaps if the planned expansion is more than 10 per cent. It might be possible to move goods through the warehouse more quickly, but it may be necessary to buy or rent additional or replacement premises. Please think of three other possible limiting factors and write them down.

Seasonal factors

Seasonal factors are not relevant in all budgets, but they are in many and it can be a bad mistake to ignore them. This is best illustrated with an example.

In the UK it is likely that a greetings card shop will achieve 25 per cent of its annual sales in the three weeks leading up to Christmas. Sales will also be above average in the months of February through to June. This is because of the so-called Spring Seasons ranges for Valentine's Day, Easter, Mother's Day and Father's Day. This will obviously affect the sales budget, but there will be other implications too. Perhaps staff costs will be higher in certain months and it will affect stock purchases, borrowing and bank interest.

SUNDAY

MONDAY

TUESDAY

WEDNESDAY

THURSDAY

FRIDAY

SATURDAY

Summary

Today we have:

- Looked at the differences between plans, budgets and forecasts and why the differences are important.
- Seen why budgets and forecasts are important.
- Considered whether budgets and forecasts should be easily achievable or prepared on an optimistic basis.
- Looked at the different approaches to preparing budgets and forecasts.
- Examined the importance of limiting factors, budget assumptions and other factors that must be taken into account.
- Answered some key questions.

Tomorrow we will examine different budgeting techniques. We will also look in detail at the programme for planning the budgets and forecasts, and how they are reviewed and approved.

SUNDAY

MONDAY

TUESDAY

WEDNESDAY

THURSDAY

FRIDAY

SATURDAY

Fact-check (answers at the back)

1. Must a budget always be expressed in financial terms?
   a) Yes, always ❏
   b) No, never ❏
   c) It is optional ❏
   d) Almost always ❏

2. Which of the following are advantages of preparing budgets and forecasts?
   a) It enables the organization to comply with the law ❏
   b) It gives managers information that will help them manage ❏
   c) It proves that the accounting records balance ❏
   d) All of the above ❏

3. Which of the following statements is true if completed and approved budgets are subsequently ignored?
   a) The whole exercise has been a complete waste of time ❏
   b) The budgets should be done again ❏
   c) The discipline of preparing the budgets has been of some value ❏
   d) Nothing has been lost because the whole value lies in the preparation ❏

4. Which of the following are advantages of leaving budgets to the accountants?
   a) They have got the time to do it ❏
   b) They always know a lot about budgets ❏
   c) Other managers can go home early ❏
   d) There will be no encroachment on the valuable time of the other managers ❏

5. Must budgets and forecasts always cover a period of a year?
   a) Yes ❏
   b) No and they never do ❏
   c) No – because they must cover a period of six months ❏
   d) No – but they often do ❏

6. In most people's opinion, which of the following statements are true?
   a) Budgets should be easily achievable ❏
   b) Budgets should be the midpoint of likely outcomes ❏
   c) Budgets should be ambitious but definitely achievable ❏
   d) Budgets should be extremely difficult to achieve ❏

7. Which of the following statements are suitable for inclusion in a list of budget assumptions?
a) The business will have a good year ☐
b) The business will have a disappointing year ☐
c) Customers will take an average of 60 days to pay ☐
d) All managers will be happy ☐

8. Which of the following is a limiting factor?
a) New staff are essential and they take six months to train properly ☐
b) Traffic congestion near the office is bad ☐
c) The bank manager does not like us ☐
d) The coffee machine does not work properly ☐

9. 'It is hoped that 90 per cent of our waste is recycled'. Is this:
a) a plan ☐
b) a forecast ☐
c) a budget ☐
d) none of the above? ☐

10. Should departments that have no revenue prepare expenditure budgets?
a) Definitely not ☐
b) Probably not ☐
c) Probably yes ☐
d) It's a silly question ☐

SUNDAY

MONDAY

TUESDAY

WEDNESDAY

THURSDAY

FRIDAY

SATURDAY

MONDAY

More budgeting and forecasting fundamentals

Today we start by looking at different budgeting and forecasting methods and seeing the advantages and disadvantages of each. This should help you prepare your budgets and help you decide which methods are most appropriate for your organization. We then move on to the mechanics of budget preparation, which is a big section of today's chapter and covers several aspects of the subject. Finally, there is something about the way that budgets are approved. If you are a very senior manager this is intended for you, and if you are not it may help you make a sensible case to the bosses.

The topics covered comprise:

- Incremental budgets and forecasts
- Zero-based budgets
- Flexible budgets
- Rolling budgets
- The mechanics of budget preparation
- The budget or forecast plan and timetable
- Budget approval

Incremental budgets and forecasts

Incremental budgets and forecasts use the previous year's actual figures as a basis, and then increase them or decrease them by an appropriate amount or (more usually) an appropriate percentage. At its worst this might be a single percentage applied across the board, but this would be very unsatisfactory. The variance percentage should be carefully thought out and driven by significant factors. At its very simplest, if there is going to be a rent increase of 3 per cent on the first day of the budget year, the rent budget will be increased by 3 per cent. This does not, of course, mean that all the budget figures should be increased by 3 per cent. Each item in the budget should be looked at individually. Even the rent budget might need a second look. It could be that extra premises will be rented part way through the year. Incremental budgets and forecasts have the merit of probably taking less time to prepare than some other methods.

An obvious objection to this approach is that it does not compel a thorough analysis of costs and revenue. Zero-based budgets do that and these are examined next in this chapter. On the other hand, *and with the important proviso that there is a proper review*, incremental budgeting may well be sensible. It is most likely to be useful in well-established organizations where past activity is likely to be a good starting point when forecasting the future. The approach is widely practised and likely to be used for at least part of the budgeting process.

Zero-based budgets

The philosophy of zero-based budgeting is that every part of the budget must be formulated on its merits and without reference to what has happened in the past. This differs from the more usual baseline budgeting, in which the budget may largely be based on adapting what has previously happened.

It is worth illustrating this with a very simple example. Let us suppose that last year's wage bill was £1 million. Baseline budgeting might take last year's figure plus a wage rise of 5 per cent, giving a total of £1,050,000. Zero-based budgeting, on the other hand, would mean that the justification for each employee must be examined and the expected wages of each employee must be examined. This might give a result of £1,050,000, but it might give a very different figure.

Zero-based budgeting has definite advantages. It should help identify and eliminate waste. It encourages managers to find cost-effective ways to improve operations and it may motivate them towards being innovative and more efficient. It should also encourage the efficient allocation of resources and detect inflated budgets.

Despite all this, there are major disadvantages to zero-based methods. The most obvious is the amount of time and complexity involved in the process. Without the benefit of historical or budgeted data on which to base their assumptions, managers may unnecessarily be forced to justify routine operations. Some businesses have predictable operations that vary little over time. It is neither efficient nor effective for a manager to spend a great deal of effort developing data that could be obtained quickly and accurately by extrapolating historical data.

Flexible budgets

Consider the following:

	Budget	Actual
Units sold	10,000	6,349
Units produced	10,100	6,567
Factory wages	$1,000,000	$936,117

At first glance, factory wages are $63,883 below budget, which is cause for satisfaction. However, a second and more thoughtful examination will reveal that sales and production are both massively under budget. After taking this into account, it is probably correct to conclude that factory wages were, in fact, very unsatisfactory. This illustrates an advantage of flexible budgets. In such budgets, related costs are budgeted at different levels to accommodate a range of possible outcomes. Meaningful budgets are then available to compare with actual figures, even though events may not turn out as predicted.

A flexible budget may be defined in one of two ways:

- A budget which allows for variations in cost for each selected level of output over a range of possible outputs.
- A budget which is added to and adjusted each quarter (or other period) so that there is no artificial break-off period. The cumulative results and their effect on future planning can be seen quite readily.

Rolling budgets

In the case of a fixed-period budget or forecast, a budget or forecast is, not surprisingly, prepared for a fixed period, which is often a year. Actual results are then monitored against the budget or forecast and towards the end of the period a further budget or forecast is made for the following period. This is what happens in most cases.

The principle of a rolling budget or forecast is that periodically, say quarterly, what has actually happened is consigned to history and a new budget for this period of time is added to the end of the budget. This is illustrated with the following, which shows just sales.

	Budget	Actual
January to March	£1,900,000	£2,040,000
April to June	£2,000,000	
July to September	£2,100,000	
October to December	£2,200,000	
	£8,200,000	

After or just before the end of the first quarter a sales budget for the following January to March is prepared, and the budget is then as follows:

	Budget
April to June	£2,000,000
July to September	£2,100,000
October to December	£2,200,000
January to March	£2,090,000
	£8,390,000

The mechanics of budget preparation

It is a very obvious point to make, but it is essential that everyone working on a budget or forecast is operating the same system. To use a colloquial phrase, everyone must be singing from the same hymn sheet. It would be a nonsense if some managers were using spreadsheets, some using paper forms and some using another system, though having said that it perhaps would not matter if they did their calculations in different ways and then entered the results into the same unified system.

It is usual for the accountants to decide and issue the budget forms and budgeting system that will be used. It is very desirable and perhaps even essential that the budget headings are the same as the headings that are used in the accounting system. Thus, stationery in a department's overhead budget will have the same meaning as stationery in the accounting system. Furthermore, the relationships between figures in the budget should be the same as in the accounting system. So, for example, invoiced sales will probably increase the total sales, increase the profit before tax, increase the tax charge, increase the profit after tax, affect the cash total and affect the balance sheet.

Spreadsheets do not contribute wisdom, but they are of enormous help in budget preparation. They greatly speed up the arithmetic aspects and enable 'what if?' questions to be answered almost instantly. When using spreadsheets figures are inserted into cells. Columns and formulae relationships must be carefully designed. Then a figure entered into a cell will affect other relevant figures throughout the budget or budgets.

For example, a figure entered into the overhead expenses of a department will consequently change:

- Total costs of the department
- Total costs of the organization
- Profit (or loss)
- Budgeted cash flow
- Budgeted balance sheet.

It is clear that spreadsheets, like many computer applications, save a vast amount of management time. So why do so many managers, in the UK and the USA at least, work longer than their parents and grandparents did and suffer more stress? It is a great mystery.

Now please test your understanding of this by writing down the effects of an increase in raw material prices in a manufacturing company. This might be very difficult if you have little or no accounting knowledge, so do not worry if you cannot do it. The answer is given after the summary at the end of this chapter.

The budget or forecast plan and timetable

These should be issued before the budgeting or forecasting work begins, and they should be issued by top management or by the accountants with the approval of top management. Managers should not be swamped with detail that is not relevant to them and it is possible that some information might be confidential and should not go to all managers. Redundancy intentions, for example, could come into this category. For these reasons some managers should perhaps not receive all the material. The following are examples of various budgets in a large organization, though there could be more or fewer depending on individual circumstances:

- Capital expenditure budget
- Sales budget
- Revenue budget
- Profit and loss budget
- Cash budget
- Budgeted balance sheet.

With the exception of the budgeted balance sheet all these budgets will be reviewed during the rest of the week.

It should be clear which managers are responsible for which budgets. Individual managers might have responsibility for a sector of a budget and, for example, for the expenditure of a department within the profit and loss budget.

Budget targets

The differences between top-down and bottom-up were explained yesterday. If a top-down approach is favoured, each manager will be given a target or targets that must be achieved in the budget. These will lead to an overall targeted profit (or loss) of a certain figure. There may be targets other than those within the profit and loss budget. There could, for example, be a target that total money owing by customers should never exceed the equivalent of 45 days' sales.

If a bottom-up approach is favoured, such targets will not be issued. Instead managers will be charged with the task of preparing to the best of their ability a responsible, constructive budget that is in the interests of their department and of the organization.

In practice the approach is likely to lie between these two extremes, and in my opinion this is sensible. Managers should be given some guideline targets but these should be short of rigid requirements. Managers should be trusted to act responsibly. If budget targets are issued, they could be along the following lines:

- The net profit will be at least 10 per cent higher than in the current year.
- Each department's overall costs will not be more than 4 per cent more than in the current year.
- Sales for each region will be at least 5 per cent higher than in the current year and there will be no increase in discounts allowed.
- Average stock levels will be no higher than in the current year.
- Suppliers will be paid after an average of 75 days.
- Bad debts will not be more than 2 per cent of sales.

At this point please consider whether you prefer top-down or bottom-up and give two reasons. There are no right or wrong answers so none are given at the end of the chapter.

Budget assumptions

The desirability of top management issuing budget assumptions was explained yesterday and examples of budget assumptions were listed. These should normally form part of the package given to managers.

Budget forms

This heading is perhaps a throwback to a time when budgets were done on paper and it was usual to have a budget form for each category of income and expense. Each form would have an appropriate heading and probably an identifying code number. There would be a space on each form where details of the budget calculations would be entered. These would lead to a total and there would be boxes on the form for the total to be split over months or some other appropriate period.

Perhaps the budgets will be done manually and such forms will be used, but the use of spreadsheets is much more likely. Even so, it is important that a record be kept of the calculations leading to the totals, and exactly how the totals were split into monthly divisions or divisions for some other period. These are the figures entered into the cells on the spreadsheets. Some sort of electronic record may be kept, but perhaps the forms still have their uses.

Budget timetable

The package should include a timetable for all the work to be done and the approvals given. Obviously the contents will vary from organization to organization and the number and complexity of the budgets. The following illustrates the principles for a large company and a full set of budgets.

20 March	Budget package issued
3 April	Submissions for capital expenditure budget
5 April	Submissions for sales and departmental expenditure
6 April	Board committee consideration of capital expenditure, sales and departmental expenditure submissions. Requests for revisions issued as necessary
13 April	Board committee consideration of capital expenditure budget and full profit and loss budget. Requests for revisions issued as necessary
17 April	Board committee approval of: - capital expenditure budget - profit and loss budget - cash budget - budgeted balance sheet
19 April	Full board approval of all budgets

At first sight and perhaps at second sight too, all this seems horribly bureaucratic and likely to stifle initiative. Nevertheless, a formal timetable along these lines will be necessary in a large company. There could be chaos if managers work to their own timetables without regard to the needs of other managers and the need to finish on time. Furthermore, intermediate dates are necessary because of the possible need for revisions, and because some budget calculations cannot be done until figures from other departments and budgets are available. For example, it is not possible to get the depreciation charge in the profit and loss account exactly right until details of the capital expenditure budget are known.

Having said all that, the possibilities remain that the programme and procedures may be bureaucratic and stifle initiative. Attempts should be made to minimize this. Everyone should be encouraged to talk to each other and raise problems informally, which is a good idea throughout the year anyway and does not always happen in large organizations. The whole procedure can probably be much more informal in small businesses.

Budget approval

When all the budgets are completed they should be signed off or in some way formally accepted. Perhaps this will be done by a single person such as the managing director, or perhaps by a group such as the board of directors. Hopefully the figures are satisfactory and can be readily approved, but even so the approvers should have enough knowledge to form the realistic belief that they are obtainable. If this is not the case, they should make enquiries, because they should not approve figures that they do not believe can be achieved.

This poses the question of what they should do if the figures presented to them are not satisfactory. One possibility is to order across-the-board cuts such as '10 per cent savings in all departments'. This may be tempting but in my opinion it is usually a mistake. Probably some budgets should be cut by more, and some by less or not at all. It is almost guaranteed to demotivate managers and staff, and they may decide to inflate their budget submissions next time in order to accommodate the anticipated cuts. When Ronald Reagan became Governor of California he quickly ordered such across the board budget cuts with some unfortunate consequences. However, the great man quickly realized that this was a mistake and adopted an individually tailored approach to achieve the necessary savings.

Summary

Today we have:

- Looked at different budgeting techniques and examined the advantages and disadvantages of each.
- Studied the mechanics of preparing budgets and seen the importance of the same systems being used by all concerned.
- Seen what information should be provided to get the budget work going.
- Looked at the elements of a budget timetable.
- Seen how budgets should be approved and noted a common mistake and its possible consequences.

As Julie Andrews famously sang in *The Sound of Music*, 'Let's start at the very beginning, a very good place to start'. This is what we have done yesterday and today. We are now ready to start looking at the individual budgets in detail. Tomorrow we start with the capital expenditure budget, the sales budget and the revenue budget.

SUNDAY
MONDAY
TUESDAY
WEDNESDAY
THURSDAY
FRIDAY
SATURDAY

Answer to question in the mechanics of budget preparation section

1 Cost of sales will increase
2 Gross profit will reduce
3 Net profit will reduce

Fact-check (answers at the back)

1. On what figures are incremental budgets and forecasts based?
   a) The average of the last three years' actual figures ❑
   b) The managing director's requirements ❑
   c) Last year's budget ❑
   d) Last year's actual figures ❑

2. Which of the following is a problem with incremental budgets?
   a) They take too long to prepare ❑
   b) They do not compel a thorough analysis of costs and revenue ❑
   c) They do not involve all layers of management ❑
   d) They are inherently unreliable ❑

3. Which of the following are advantages of zero-based budgeting?
   a) It should help identify and eliminate waste ❑
   b) It encourages managers to find cost-effective ways to improve operations ❑
   c) It may motivate managers to be more efficient ❑
   d) All of the above ❑

4. Which of the following is true of flexible budgets?
   a) Related costs are budgeted at different levels to accommodate a range of possible outcomes ❑
   b) The budget timetable is flexible ❑
   c) Top managers are flexible when reviewing the results ❑
   d) Actual results are never exactly the same as the budgeted results ❑

5. Which of the following is true of rolling budgets?
   a) They are suitable for managers who cannot get it right first time ❑
   b) As a new period is added an old period is dropped off ❑
   c) You do not need to monitor the actual results against the budget ❑
   d) They have fallen out of favour and are hardly ever done ❑

6. Do spreadsheets contribute wisdom?
   a) Yes ❑
   b) No ❑
   c) Sometimes ❑
   d) It all depends ❑

7. Who should issue the budget or forecast plan and timetable?
a) No one – it should emerge spontaneously ❑
b) The accountants ❑
c) Top management ❑
d) Everyone should issue their own ❑

8. Are budget targets always provided to managers?
a) Yes ❑
b) No ❑
c) Yes – but they should not be ❑
d) No – but they should be ❑

9. Which of the following is a likely disadvantage of arbitrary, across-the-board budget cuts?
a) They do not work ❑
b) They demotivate managers ❑
c) Computer systems probably cannot cope with them ❑
d) They have been condemned by the Institute of Personnel Managers ❑

10. Which of the following budgets will be affected by an increase in revenue?
a) The profit and loss budget ❑
b) The cashflow budget ❑
c) The budgeted balance sheet ❑
d) All of the above ❑

SUNDAY

MONDAY

TUESDAY

WEDNESDAY

THURSDAY

FRIDAY

SATURDAY

TUESDAY

Capital expenditure, sales and revenue budgets

During the first two days of this week we have reconnoitred the subject of budgets and forecasts. We have explored various principles and aspects, answered some fundamental questions and looked at different budgeting and forecasting methods. It is now time to start looking at the different budgets in detail, and to do a budgeting exercise which hopefully you will not find too difficult. The three budgets that we cover today are important in their own right and are essential steps in preparing the overall profit and loss budget. They are the three headings in this chapter, namely:

- Capital expenditure budget
- Sales budget
- Revenue budget

Capital expenditure budget

Capital expenditure is money spent on assets that are intended to be held and which will provide continuing benefits to the business. The assets are expected to retain some or all of their value over an extended period, which is usually taken to be more than a year. This is as opposed to stock which will be resold, or raw materials or components which will be used in manufacturing. It also excludes items which will be quickly used, such as stationery. In practice there must be a minimum value before something is classed as capital expenditure. This will vary from business to business, but it could well be about £500 for an individual item. For example, a toaster for the office kitchen retains some of its value and provides benefits in the long term, but its value is too small for it to be classified as capital expenditure.

Most capital items do steadily lose their value, but over a period of more than a year. This may be as a result of wear and tear, the passage of time or obsolescence. The accounting treatment is to put capital expenditure into the balance sheet, then drip feed a depreciation charge into the profit and loss account over a suitable number of years. Budgeting should follow this accounting practice, which is one reason why a separate capital expenditure budget is needed. Commonly identified categories of capital expenditure and typical rules for their depreciation are as follows:

Category of fixed asset	Depreciation charge
Freehold land and buildings	Nil or 2 per cent per year
Leasehold land and buildings	Over the life of the lease
Plant and machinery	25 per cent per year
Computers	25 per cent per year
Motor vehicles	25 per cent per year
Fixtures and fittings	10 per cent per year

The capital expenditure budget is extremely important in some companies. The big oil companies such as Shell and BP come to mind, and also big manufacturing companies such as Rolls Royce. In their cases the capital expenditure budget could total billions. It is much less important in many other companies and may be virtually non-existent in small service companies, though any company cars should not be overlooked.

It is important to get the timing right. Expenditure on a big project may be over a number of months or an even longer period. Cash will be affected as money is spent, but depreciation usually only starts when the project is completed. If plant and machinery is depreciated over four years, a new machine costing $400,000 will result in a charge of $100,000 to the revenue expenditure budget if it is budgeted for day one of the annual budget. If, on the other hand, it is budgeted for the first day of the tenth month, the depreciation charge will be only $25,000.

 If the figures in the capital expenditure budget are really significant, it may be desirable to budget for known items individually and then add a contingency for each month.

Managers should be prepared, and perhaps required, to justify their budget proposals in detail. If proposed capital expenditure is high, and especially if cash is tight, the capital expenditure budget is likely to be scrutinized very carefully by top management. This is because it may be a place where big cuts may be made. Perhaps the expenditure is not really essential or perhaps it can wait a bit longer. Must company cars really be replaced this year? I once worked for a company where capital expenditure was high and cash was always tight. To the annoyance of the managers, a very expensive item of capital expenditure had been cut from the budget in six successive years, even though it was justified by investment criteria. When I left, it was in the budget for the seventh time and it looked as though it would at last survive the cuts.

The following shows how a typical capital expenditure budget may be laid out. In practice there may well be some supporting notes to justify each item of expenditure. There may also be a separate section showing anticipated receipts from the sale of existing capital items.

Capital expenditure budget for the six months to 30 June

	Jan £000s	Feb £000s	March £000s	April £000s	May £000s	June £000s	Total £000s
Leasehold land and buildings							
New office in Windsor						900	900
						900	900
Computers							
Ref. Project Swindon	50	50	50				150
Ref. Project Reading	10	10	60	60	20		160
Contingency	5	5	5	5	5	5	30
	65	65	115	65	25	5	340
Motor cars							
Replacement cars for directors			40	70	50		160
Replacement cars for sales staff	75	75					150
New pool car						15	15
	75	75	40	70	50	15	325
Fixtures and fittings							
Contingency	4	4	4	4	4	4	24
	4	4	4	4	4	4	24
Total capital expenditure	144	144	159	139	79	924	1,589

Sales budget

It is understandable if you think that the sales budget should be the same as the revenue budget. It sometimes is, but more often it is not. This is because there is usually a period of time between taking an order and fulfilling it. In the case of a retail shop that does not give credit, the sales budget may be the same as the revenue budget, but even here there will be a timing difference if goods are out of stock and ordered for customers. The sales budget reflects expected orders taken. These orders should be reflected in the revenue budget only at the point where it is expected that deliveries will be made or services performed. The effect on cash is different again and this usually happens later still.

The sales budget should be one of the first budgets done. This is because it affects the other budgets and these cannot be finalized until the budgeted sales are known. If other budgets are prepared without this information, there is a risk that the budgets may be unbalanced. For example the budget for overheads may be expanded to cope with an additional volume of sales that will not be in the sales budget. Of course all this may be spotted and corrected when the budgets are reviewed, but it is better to get it right first time.

The sales budget is a very important one because so much else depends on it. A company that has no sales has no business, and a company that only has small sales only has a small business. The rest of the company must budget to support the level of sales that will be budgeted, with production (or purchases for resale) and perhaps overheads expanding if the sales budget indicates increased activity. The reverse is, of course, true if the sales budget indicates reduced activity.

The sales budget may be harder to do than the expenditure budgets. This is because expenditure is, or at least should be, largely within the control of the managers. The sales and marketing effort will have a big influence on the level of sales, but there will be other important factors as well. Obviously these include the sales effort of competitors, together with their pricing structure and marketing strategy. Also to be considered are the general economic climate and a host of other things, perhaps even including the weather. That is not easy to forecast a year in advance. Sir Stuart Rose of the major retail chain Marks & Spencer once said that he did not like using the weather as an excuse, but it was hard to hit sales targets when customers had to use boats to get to the stores.

We will now see how a sales budget is laid out. It can be done in several ways but the following is a good example and covers a period of six months to 30 June. We will assume that a company's sales force is organized into two regions (southern and northern) and that it also makes exports. We will also assume that it has two products (A and B). A sells for $20 in the southern and northern regions and for $25 in the export market. B sells for $40 in the southern and northern regions and for $45 in the export market.

After a lot of work the assumptions for the sales budget have been fixed as follows:

Southern region	
Product A	1,000 units in each of the six months
Product B	1,200 units in January, then an increase of 50 units per month in each of the following months

Northern region	
Product A	1,350 units in January, February and March, then 1,160 units in each of the remaining three months
Product B	3,600 units in January, February and March, then an increase of 100 units per month in each of the following months

Exports

	Product A	Product B
January	300 units	200 units
February	300 units	200 units
March	2,000 units	200 units
April	300 units	200 units
May	600 units	200 units
June	400 units	200 units

This can be summarized in financial terms as follows:

Sales budget for six months to 30 June

	Jan $	Feb $	March $	April $	May $	June $	Total $
Southern region							
Product A	20,000	20,000	20,000	20,000	20,000	20,000	120,000
Product B	48,000	50,000	52,000	54,000	56,000	58,000	318,000
	68,000	70,000	72,000	74,000	76,000	78,000	438,000
Northern region							
Product A	27,000	27,000	27,000	23,200	23,200	23,200	150,600
Product B	144,000	144,000	144,000	148,000	152,000	156,000	888,000
	171,000	171,000	171,000	171,200	175,200	179,200	1,038,600
Exports							
Product A	7,500	7,500	50,000	7,500	15,000	10,000	97,500
Product B	9,000	9,000	9,000	9,000	9,000	9,000	54,000
	16,500	16,500	59,000	16,500	24,000	19,000	151,500
Total sales	255,500	257,500	302,000	261,700	275,200	276,200	1,628,100

The same information can be summarized in two other ways. If it is wished to show it by product, the total split is as follows:

Product A	$368,100
Product B	$1,260,000
	$1,628,100

If it is wished to separate the home market from exports, the total split is:

Home market	$1,476,600
Exports	$151,500
	$1,628,100

Revenue budget

The revenue budget is the income that appears as the top line or top section of the profit and loss budget. It corresponds with invoiced sales to customers and invoices are usually issued when goods are delivered or services performed. However, this is not always the case. Two exceptions come to mind:

- A contract where services are performed over a period but payment is required in advance. Insurance is an example and in this case payment is often required at the beginning of the period covered by the insurance.
- Stage payments during the progress of a building contract.

The next example ignores these possible complications and you are asked to convert the sales budget in the last section of this chapter into the revenue budget. You may use the blank form as a template and you can check your answer against the one at the end of this chapter.

You need to know that customers in the southern and northern regions are invoiced an average of 30 days after their orders have been placed. Export customers are invoiced an average of 60 days after their orders have been placed. Sales in the three months before the period covered by the sales budget were as follows:

	Oct $	Nov $	Dec $
Southern region			
Product A	18,107	20,134	19,726
Product B	38,111	41,296	46,344
Northern region			
Product A	26,004	26,238	26,467
Product B	145,211	99,687	151,999
Exports			
Product A	44,372	6,087	8,331
Product B	7,824	9,235	8,477

Revenue budget for six months to 30 June

	Jan $	Feb $	March $	April $	May $	June $	Total $
Southern region							
Product A							
Product B							
Northern region							
Product A							
Product B							
Exports							
Product A							
Product B							
Total sales							

Summary

Today we have:

● Looked in detail at capital expenditure budgets and seen why, in some cases at least, they are very important. We have seen how a typical capital expenditure budget is prepared.

● Looked at sales budgets, which are always very important.

● Seen how a sales budget is turned into a revenue budget. Finally, you should have used information provided to set out a revenue budget.

Tomorrow and Thursday we deal with the profit and loss budget, starting with the expenditure part of it tomorrow. More managers contribute to this than any of the other budgets. It is the most recognized and many consider it to be the most important.

SUNDAY

MONDAY

TUESDAY

WEDNESDAY

THURSDAY

FRIDAY

SATURDAY

Answer to revenue budget for six months to 30 June

	Jan $	Feb $	March $	April $	May $	June $	Total $
Southern region							
Product A	19,726	20,000	20,000	20,000	20,000	20,000	119,726
Product B	46,344	48,000	50,000	52,000	54,000	56,000	306,344
	66,070	68,000	70,000	72,000	74,000	76,000	426,070
Northern region							
Product A	26,467	27,000	27,000	27,000	23,200	23,200	153,867
Product B	151,999	144,000	144,000	144,000	148,000	152,000	883,999
	178,466	171,000	171,000	171,000	171,200	175,200	1,037,866
Exports							
Product A	6,087	8,331	7,500	7,500	50,000	7,500	86,918
Product B	9,235	8,477	9,000	9,000	9,000	9,000	53,712
	15,322	16,808	16,500	16,500	59,000	16,500	140,630
Total sales	259,858	255,808	257,500	259,500	304,200	267,700	1,604,566

Fact-check (answers at the back)

1. Which of the following is capital expenditure?
   a) Purchase of goods for resale ❑
   b) Bank interest ❑
   c) Purchase of company cars ❑
   d) Payment of wages ❑

2. £300,000 is paid to lease a building for six years. What should be the depreciation charge for the first full year?
   a) £50,000 ❑
   b) Nothing ❑
   c) £150,000 ❑
   d) £300,000 plus associated legal expenses ❑

3. Over what period is it usually considered that an asset must retain at least some of its value for it to be considered (subject to conditions) to be capital expenditure?
   a) More than six months ❑
   b) More than a year ❑
   c) More than two years ❑
   d) Indefinitely ❑

4. Can the sales budget be the same as the revenue budget?
   a) Yes – and it almost always is ❑
   b) Yes – but it does not often happen ❑
   c) No ❑
   d) Only in the engineering industry ❑

5. What goes into the revenue budget?
   a) Orders already taken and orders expected to be taken, provided that they will both be invoiced in the budget period ❑
   b) Orders budgeted to be taken in the budget period ❑
   c) Orders taken before the start of the budget period ❑
   d) Orders that will be taken in the budget period, but which will not be invoiced until after the budget period ❑

6. When should the sales budget be done?
   a) It does not matter ❑
   b) It should be one of the first budgets done ❑
   c) It should be one of the last budgets done ❑
   d) It should be done at the same time as all the other budgets ❑

7. Why may the sales budget be hard to get right?
   a) Sales managers are bad at budgeting ❑
   b) The assumption in the question is mistaken. Sales budgets are actually easy to get right ❑
   c) A lot may depend on what competitors do ❑
   d) None of the above ❑

8. Which of the following usually go into the capital expenditure budget?
a) Computers ☐
b) Plant and machinery ☐
c) Fixtures and fittings ☐
d) All of the above ☐

9. When should a motor car be entered into the capital expenditure budget?
a) When it is ordered ☐
b) When it is delivered and accepted ☐
c) When it is paid for ☐
d) When it is first driven ☐

10. Which of the following is not a factor in setting the sales budget?
a) The expected spend on advertising ☐
b) Competitors' pricing policy ☐
c) The depreciation charge ☐
d) Our pricing policy ☐

SUNDAY

MONDAY

TUESDAY

WEDNESDAY

THURSDAY

FRIDAY

SATURDAY

WEDNESDAY

Expenditure budgets

Many managers will identify most closely with the expenditure budget, perhaps together with the profit and loss budget. This is because it is the one to which they are most likely to contribute and the one against which their performance is most likely to be measured. You may therefore see this chapter as being particularly relevant. It is likely that there will be a separate expenditure mini-budget for each cost centre or department, and that these will be aggregated together to show the wider picture.

The programme today is:

- The organization of the expenditure budget
- An example of an expenditure budget
- Expenditure budget exercise

The organization of the expenditure budget

In a small and uncomplicated organization the structure and layout of the expenditure budget will be straightforward. It is just a simple listing of all the categories of expenditure, with appropriate figures and the total. It will probably look like the following:

	Last year's budget £	Last year's actual £	This year's budget £
Expense category 1			
Expense category 2			
Expense category 3			
Expense category 4			
Expense category 5			
Expense category 6			
Expense category 7			
Expense category 8			
Total			

In practice there would almost certainly be more expense categories than just eight, and the budget would probably be spread over 12 monthly periods or divided in some other way. Last year's budget and last year's actual may or may not be shown. They do help when the figures are prepared and reviewed. The headings pose the obvious question of how (unless the budget is prepared after the start of the period that it covers) last year's actual can be known. Of course it cannot be known, but estimates would be inserted based on the latest available information.

This is for a small and uncomplicated organization, and the one form would possibly cover the whole business, though the expense categories might be grouped in some way. The form and headings would probably be similar in a large and complicated business, though there would be many forms and not just one. There would be a form for each cost centre or department, and the expense categories would be appropriate to that department. For example a heading for 'Advertising' would be on the form for the marketing or sales department, and a heading for 'Staff Recruitment Costs' would be on the form for the human resources department.

The budgets for the cost centres or departments might go straight into the profit and loss budget, but depending on the complexity of the organization they might be grouped in some way into functions or divisions. For example in a big company the sales department budgets might be grouped as follows:

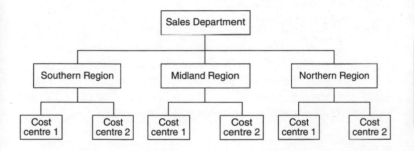

The expenditure budget for each region would be the aggregation of the expenditure budgets for the two cost centres within it. The expenditure budget for the whole sales department would be the aggregation of the expenditure budgets for the three regions. Assuming that there is an overall manager for the whole sales department, a manager for each region and a manager for each cost centre, ten different managers would have responsibility for some or all of the sales department's expenditure budget. No doubt the sales department manager and the three regional managers would review each of the budgets for which they had responsibility, and perhaps request or require that changes be made.

An example of an expenditure budget

It is now time to see an example of how an expenditure budget is prepared. The budget form contains 11 categories of expense. These have been chosen to show how a range of budget calculations might be made, not as a likely real-life department or cost centre. There are few absolutely right or wrong figures because a budget is an individual interpretation of policy and available information. You might see some of the figures differently.

The following is a list of budget assumptions issued by the managing director, together with some available and relevant information. This is followed by the completed budget form, then a note of many of the budget calculations is given.

Salaries

The current payroll (including employers' National Insurance contributions) is £1,282,441 per year. It is assumed that on 1 July there will be an average pay rise of 5 per cent. It is also assumed that redundancies on 1 October will save £80,000 per year and that one-off redundancy payments will be £23,000.

Rent

There will be a £15,000 per year increase on 1 January.

Postage

It is believed that there will be an overall 20 per cent reduction in postal use and that the reduction will gather pace during the year. It is also assumed that there will be no increase in postal charges during the year.

(Comment – in view of increases in recent years, could this last assumption perhaps be rather optimistic?)

Telephone

It is believed that a 5 per cent reduction on current costs will be achieved throughout the year.

Depreciation

The depreciation rate on company cars is 25 per cent per year, and on fixtures and fittings it is 10 per cent per year. The balance sheet position at 31 December is as follows:

	Company cars £	Fixtures and fittings £
Cost	210,000	40,000
Less depreciation to date	110,000	10,000
Net book value	100,000	30,000

The capital expenditure budget shows purchases of cars for £150,000 on 1 January and fixtures and fittings for £10,000 on 1 January. There are no plans to sell any fixed assets. All the company cars are less than three years old.

Bad debts

The managing director has instructed that an additional bad debt reserve of £7,000 per month should be budgeted.

Travel expenses

It is believed that these can be held at the level for last year.

Hotel costs

It is believed that these can be held at the level for last year.

Stationery

The managing director believes that both last year's budget and last year's actual are absurdly high. He has required a cut of 50 per cent on last year's budget.

Bank interest

It is believed that average borrowing over the coming year will be:

- Quarter 1   £850,000
- Quarter 2   £920,000

SUNDAY MONDAY TUESDAY WEDNESDAY THURSDAY FRIDAY SATURDAY

- Quarter 3   £990,000
- Quarter 4   £900,000

It is believed that the interest rate throughout the year will be 10 per cent.

Audit fee

The managing director believes that the auditors give a terrible service and charge too much, and he is annoyed that last year's actual charge is significantly over budget. He has demanded a cut of 25 per cent on last year's budget.

It is company practice to accrue the expected audit fee evenly through the year.

(Comment – the managing director is surely mistaken. All auditors give a good service and charge moderate fees.)

Expenditure budget for the year to 31 December

	Last year's budget £	Last year's actual £	Quarter 1 £	Quarter 2 £	Quarter 3 £	Quarter 4 £	Budget for total year £
Salaries	1,230,000	1,269,111	321,000	321,000	337,000	340,000	1,319,000
Rent	205,000	205,000	55,000	55,000	55,000	55,000	220,000
Postage	22,000	26,117	6,000	5,300	5,200	4,500	21,000
Telephone	34,500	39,282	9,350	9,350	9,350	9,350	37,400
Depreciation	120,000	120,000	23,750	23,750	23,750	23,750	95,000

(continued)

Bad debts	60,000	76,398	21,000	21,000	21,000	21,000	84,000
Travel expenses	92,000	99,904	25,000	25,000	25,000	25,000	100,000
Hotel costs	84,000	92,317	23,000	23,000	23,000	23,000	92,000
Stationery	62,000	66,218	7,750	7,750	7,750	7,750	31,000
Bank interest	50,000	73,007	21,250	23,000	24,750	22,500	91,500
Audit fee	20,000	28,500	3,750	3,750	3,750	3,750	15,000
	1,979,500	2,095,854	516,850	517,900	535,550	535,600	2,105,900

Reasonable rounding of figures has been done throughout the calculations.

Salaries

- Quarter 1: At the current rate – £321,000
- Quarter 2: At the current rate – £321,000
- Quarter 3: At the current rate plus 5 per cent – £337,000
- Quarter 4: As per Quarter 3 less £20,000 plus £23,000 – £340,000

Postage

Eighty per cent of £26,117 is £20,893. After rounding and allowing for the reduction to be greater towards the end of the year this is split as shown.

Telephone

Ninety-five per cent of £39,282 is £37,317. This is allocated evenly throughout the budget period.

Depreciation

	Company cars £	Fixtures and fittings £
Original cost	210,000	40,000
Add budgeted purchases	150,000	10,000
	360,000	50,000

(continued)

	Company cars £	Fixtures and fittings £
25 per cent depreciation on company cars		90,000
10 per cent depreciation on fixtures and fittings		5,000
		95,000

Bank interest

Quarter 1: 25 per cent × 10 per cent × £850,000 = £21,250
Quarter 2: 25 per cent × 10 per cent × £920,000 = £23,000
Quarter 3: 25 per cent × 10 per cent × £990,000 = £24,750
Quarter 4: 25 per cent × 10 per cent × £900,000 = £22,500
£91,500

Expenditure budget exercise

It is now time for you to prepare an expenditure budget from information provided. Once again the categories of expense have been chosen to show a range of expenses and not to reflect a real-life department or cost centre. The following is a list of budget assumptions issued by the managing director, together with some available and relevant information. The completed form followed by a note of some of the calculations is given at the end of the chapter, but please fill in the blank form that follows before looking.

Overall approach

The directors are disappointed with last year's performance and the failure to achieve budget. They demand a rigorous approach to budgeting expenses and that last year's poor performance is not used as an excuse for unjustified expenditure this year.

Salaries

The payroll (including employers' National Insurance contributions) has averaged £232,000 per month in the last three months. There must be a total freeze on overtime, which will save £8,000 per month. In addition, an employee who is paid (including employers' National Insurance contributions) £60,000 a year will retire on 30 June and will not be replaced. There will be no pay increases during the year.

Computer costs

A planned project starting in March must be deferred until November and the budget must be for ongoing costs of £4,000 per month. The new project is expected to cost £35,000 spread evenly over five months and this will be additional to the ongoing work.

Property costs

The directors want a 10 per cent cut in last year's actual figures.

Office costs

The directors believe that last year's budget was realistic and note that it was achieved. They suggest that the same budget figure is used.

Bad debts

The directors recognize that it was a mistake to make no provision in last year's budget. They have asked for a budget of 1 per cent of turnover. The revenue budget is as follows:

- Quarter 1   £3,300,000
- Quarter 2   £3,800,000
- Quarter 3   £4,100,000
- Quarter 4   £3,900,000

Travel

The directors think that last year's budget was too high and that the actual expenditure was disgraceful. They have asked for a budget of £105,000.

Entertainment

The directors think that the overrun on last year's budget was not justified, even though they did quite a bit of the entertaining. They want a repeat of last year's budget.

Audit fee

The directors would like a big cut but recognize that this is not realistic. They have asked for a token cut of £2,000. The audit fee should be budgeted evenly over the whole year.

Expenditure budget for the year to 31 December

	Last year's budget £	Last year's actual £	Quarter 1 £	Quarter 2 £	Quarter 3 £	Quarter 4 £	Budget for total year £
Salaries	2,640,000	2,761,134					
Computer costs	88,000	107,922					
Property costs	107,000	121,844					
Office costs	94,000	92,316					
Bad debts	–	177,431					
Travel	136,000	162,908					
Entertainment	92,000	131,111					
Audit fee	50,000	50,000					
	3,207,000	3,604,666					

Summary

Today we have:

● Looked at the structure and layout of the expenditure budget. We have seen that this may be a simple one-page document in a small organization, but more typically will be separate mini-expenditure budgets for different departments or cost centres. These are then aggregated into the whole, perhaps with intervening levels for such units as divisions or regions.

● Looked in detail at how an expenditure budget is prepared and seen an example.

Finally you will, I hope, have successfully prepared an expenditure budget from information provided.

The expenditure budget is very important in its own right, but more than that it is an essential step towards preparing the profit and loss budget. This gives the budgeted overall profit or loss and it is what we will study tomorrow.

SUNDAY
MONDAY
TUESDAY
WEDNESDAY
THURSDAY
FRIDAY
SATURDAY

Answer to expenditure budget for the year to 31 December

	Last year's budget £	Last year's actual £	Quarter 1 £	Quarter 2 £	Quarter 3 £	Quarter 4 £	Budget for total year £
Salaries	2,640,000	2,761,134	672,000	672,000	657,000	657,000	2,658,000
Computer costs	88,000	107,922	12,000	12,000	12,000	26,000	62,000
Property costs	107,000	121,844	27,500	27,500	27,500	27,500	110,000
Office costs	94,000	92,316	23,500	23,500	23,500	23,500	94,000
Bad debts	–	177,431	33,000	38,000	41,000	39,000	151,000
Travel	136,000	162,908	26,250	26,250	26,250	26,250	105,000
Entertainment	92,000	131,111	23,000	23,000	23,000	23,000	92,000
Audit fee	50,000	50,000	12,000	12,000	12,000	12,000	48,000
	3,207,000	3,604,666	829,250	834,250	822,250	834,250	3,320,000

Salaries

Quarter 1: £224,000 × 3 = £672,000
Quarter 2: £224,000 × 3 = £672,000
Quarter 3: £224,000 × 3 = £672,000 less
£15,000 = £657,000
Quarter 4: £224,000 × 3 = £672,000 less
£15,000 = £657,000

Computer costs

Quarter 1: 3 × £4,000 = £12,000
Quarter 2: 3 × £4,000 = £12,000
Quarter 3: 3 × £4,000 = £12,000
Quarter 4: 3 × £4,000 = £12,000 plus £14,000 = £26,000

Fact-check (answers at the back)

1. What should be put into the 'Last year's actual' column when the budget is prepared before the end of last year?
   a) Last year's budget ☐
   b) Nothing ☐
   c) The best estimate of what last year's actual will be ☐
   d) Twice the actual figures for the first six months of last year ☐

2. Why will most managers identify particularly closely with the expenditure budget?
   a) It is the one to which they are most likely to contribute ☐
   b) It is the one against which they are most likely to be measured ☐
   c) It is important and probably readily understood ☐
   d) All of the above ☐

3. For what should there be a separate expenditure budget form?
   a) The whole company ☐
   b) The whole division ☐
   c) The whole department ☐
   d) For each cost centre if there is more than one cost centre in a department ☐

4. Is the capital expenditure budget a factor when the expenditure budget is prepared?
   a) Yes, always (if there is capital expenditure) ☐
   b) Sometimes ☐
   c) Not usually ☐
   d) No ☐

5. Is the amount of borrowing a factor when the expenditure budget is prepared?
   a) Yes, always (if there is borrowing) ☐
   b) Sometimes ☐
   c) Not usually ☐
   d) No ☐

6. In the UK are employers' National Insurance contributions a factor when the expenditure budget is prepared?
   a) No ☐
   b) Yes ☐
   c) Only in Scotland ☐
   d) Only if the business is making a profit ☐

7. Last year's budget for salaries was £1,000,000 and last year's actual was £1,200,000. The managing director's budget assumptions call for a 10 per cent increase in salaries from the first day of the budget year. You practise zero-based budgeting. What should the budget be?
   a) £1,000,000 ☐
   b) £1,200,000 ☐
   c) £1,320,000 ☐
   d) You should take account of the 10 per cent increase but examine if the employment of each worker is justified and budget accordingly ☐

8. The revenue budget shows a significant decrease in turnover compared with last year. Does it follow that there should be a corresponding reduction in the expenditure budget?
   a) No, but the possibility should be very seriously considered ☐
   b) Certainly not ☐
   c) Yes ☐
   d) Of course ☐

9. Why (in the writer's opinion) is an arbitrary, across-the-board 20 per cent cut in all expenditure budgets a bad idea?
   a) It demotivates managers ☐
   b) It makes it more likely that managers will inflate future budget submissions ☐
   c) Both of the above ☐
   d) Such cuts can never be achieved ☐

10. Where does the total of the expenditure budget go?
    a) Nowhere ☐
    b) Into the profit and loss budget ☐
    c) Into the budgeted balance sheet ☐
    d) Into the sales budget ☐

THURSDAY

The profit and loss budget

What is the most frequently asked question about budgets and forecasts? Strong contenders are 'What's the profit going to be?' or if things are not looking good 'Just how bad is it – how big is the loss?' It is the profit and loss budget or forecast that will answer these questions. They bring together into one summary all the budgeted or forecast figures of an income or expense nature (as opposed to those of an asset or liability nature). The figure at the bottom will answer these anxious questions.

The profit and loss budget therefore cannot fail to be interesting and important and this is what we study today. Taxation gets a mention for the first time this week and we look at break-even point and break-even charts. These are perhaps the most advanced part of our week's work.

The topics covered today comprise:

- Where do the figures come from?
- The format of the profit and loss budget
- Taxation
- The profit and loss budget of a trading business
- The profit and loss budget of a manufacturing business
- Break-even point and break-even charts

Where do the figures come from?

The profit and loss account is a summary of all the accounts of an income or expense nature in the bookkeeping system. This is as opposed to assets or liabilities, which go into the balance sheet. It follows that the profit and loss budget is a summary of all budgeted income and expense.

In a very small and simple operation some of the figures might go straight into the profit and loss budget without touching a subsidiary budget, but it is very much more likely that each line is taken from the total of one of the other budgets. For example, the total of the expenditure budget may go into the profit and loss budget with a heading such as 'Expenditure'. However, it is more probable that the profit and loss budget will list several departments or cost centres. The figure for each of these departments or cost centres will be taken from the relevant sections of the expenditure budget. This is how it is done in the example that follows shortly in this chapter.

The format of the profit and loss budget

Budgets are not normally intended for publication so there is a great deal of freedom about the format. The profit and loss budget should be laid out in a way that is readily understood and most useful for managers. There are extra factors for a trading business and a manufacturing business, and there is more about them later in this chapter. There may be complications in other businesses too, but the following is an example of a profit and loss budget in a simple and straightforward company. It is a consultancy that sells its services, not a physical product.

Profit and loss budget for year to 31 December

	Last year's budget $	Last year's actual $	Quarter 1 $	Quarter 2 $	Quarter 3 $	Quarter 4 $	Total year $
Sales	7,456,000	7,184,296	1,742,000	1,800,000	1,810,000	1,860,000	7,212,000
Less direct costs	3,718,000	3,722,199	853,000	936,000	940,000	1,004,000	3,733,000
	3,738,000	3,462,097	889,000	864,000	870,000	856,000	3,479,000
Directors	422,000	461,782	115,000	115,000	118,000	119,000	467,000
Sales and Marketing Department	791,000	834,664	192,000	193,000	197,000	202,000	784,000
Finance Department	401,000	398,213	98,000	98,000	102,000	103,000	401,000
Personnel Department	266,000	279,463	65,000	65,000	65,000	65,000	260,000
Administration Department	287,000	297,185	73,000	68,000	68,000	68,000	277,000
Total other costs	2,167,000	2,271,307	543,000	539,000	550,000	557,000	2,189,000
Net profit	1,571,000	1,190,790	346,000	325,000	320,000	299,000	1,290,000

This may seem a short and simple document for a company with a turnover in excess of $7 million a year, but of course there will be other detailed budgets in support of it. The sales figures at the top of the profit and loss budget are sales that are budgeted to be invoiced to customers in the periods indicated, and not orders that are budgeted to be taken at these times. They therefore come from the revenue budget and not the sales budget. The top line is sometimes called 'Turnover', which is another name for invoiced sales.

The direct costs will be the salaries and other costs (travel, etc.) of the consultants who are providing services to the customers and generating the revenue. This will be a cost centre, or perhaps the sum of several cost centres with an expenditure budget for each one. Similarly, there will be expenditure budgets for the departments shown and perhaps more than one cost centre within each department.

Having said that, and although it is not shown in the example, one or more things do sometimes go into the budgeted profit and loss account that are not in any other budget, though they will of course always affect the budgeted balance sheet. Interest payable and investment income are two of the main ones. In the example just given they might go into Finance Department or Administration Department, but they would probably not be a good fit. Apart from anything else, they probably would not be under the control of the managers heading these departments.

Taxation

The US statesman and inventor Benjamin Franklin wrote 'in this world nothing can be certain except death and taxes'. He was surely right and we have not so far mentioned taxation, so it is now time to do so.

It is almost universal practice to disregard sales tax or value added tax (VAT) in the profit and loss budget and indeed the profit and loss account. It is of course very important, and affects the cash budget and budgeted balance sheet, but any such tax collected is eventually paid over to the tax authority. It is possible to show the sales figures including tax and then deduct the tax to give the sales figures excluding tax, but it is not necessary and hardly anyone does it.

Tax on profits is another matter. In the UK this will be corporation tax for a company and income tax for a sole trader or partnership. Sometimes the view is taken that as the profit and loss budget is for the managers, and as taxation is beyond their control, it should be left out. However, it is important that at least the senior managers know the budgeted profit or loss after tax, and it is of course very important in preparing the budgeted balance sheet.

Taxation is not shown in the budgeted profit and loss account just given, but assuming corporation tax of 26 per cent the last three lines for the total year would be:

Net profit before tax	$1,290,000
Less tax	$335,400
Net profit after tax	$954,600

Before leaving the subject it is worth mentioning that Benjamin Franklin, although brilliant, was sometimes known to take risks. He invented the lightning rod and is believed to have tested it by flying a kite in a thunderstorm. Fortunately he lived to tell the tale.

The profit and loss budget of a trading business

The example earlier in this chapter was for a business that sold just its services, so we will now consider the extra factor for a business that sells goods. You probably already know that it is a bad mistake to put the costs of goods purchased for resale into the profit and loss budget at the time that the purchases are made. What should happen is that the costs of the goods actually invoiced to customers should go into the profit and loss budget, and they should do so in the same period that the revenue is recognized. The top section of the profit and loss budget will look like this:

Sales	£
Less cost of sales	£
Gross profit	£

The other costs will then be deducted and the final figure will be the net profit or loss.

The point about the timing is illustrated by the following example. It assumes that only one product is sold and that the selling price is always exactly twice the purchase price.

	Purchases £	Sales £	Cost of Sales £
January	2,405,000	1,020,000	510,000
February	1,996,000	1,310,000	655,000
March	1,721,000	968,000	484,000
April	234,000	2,324,000	1,162,000

Of course in real life it is not likely to be as simple as that. There will almost certainly be a range of products sold at a range of prices, and purchases will probably be from a range of suppliers at a range of prices.

The profit and loss budget of a manufacturing business

This is more complicated than the profit and loss budget of a trading company. It is similar in that physical goods are sold, but they are not purchased in a ready-to-sell condition. However, the top section of the profit and loss budget will look the same, namely:

Sales	£
Less cost of sales	£
Gross profit	£

The cost of sales will be the sum of everything spent to manufacture the goods that are sold. These costs will include direct wages, raw materials, purchased components and semi-manufactured goods, and manufacturing costs. The accounting system should be organized so that all the manufacturing costs can be identified. The profit and loss budget should follow this with various departments and cost centres that can be grouped and totalled to find the total cost of sales. It is likely that the use of standard costs will play a significant part in this. Most manufacturing businesses have a separate manufacturing budget for the total costs of manufacture.

As with the profit and loss budget of a trading business, the costs of the goods actually invoiced to customers should go into the profit and loss budget, and they should do so in the same period that the revenue is recognized.

Break-even point and break-even charts

It is extremely useful to know the budgeted level of sales at which break-even will be achieved. This is the point at which the costs exactly equal the revenues, and a break-even chart can show this. Furthermore, it can show the level of profit or loss at any particular level of sales. In order to do this, it is necessary to know:

● The amount of fixed costs
● The amount of variable costs per unit of sale
● The sales price per unit.

Fixed costs are costs that stay the same regardless of the level of sales. Office rent is a good example. In practice it may be very difficult or impossible to identify all the factors accurately. Some costs may be semi-variable and fixed costs may increase once a certain level of sales is reached. Various other problems may be encountered. Having made these qualifications, let us see how it works with a simple example.

A company imports and sells clocks. It pays $5.00 for each clock and the selling price per clock is $10.00. The company has fixed costs of $200,000.

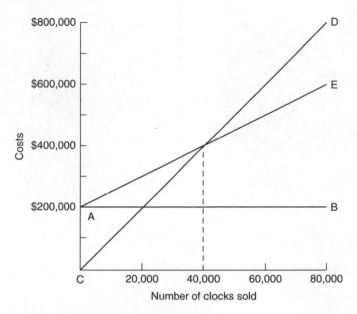

The vertical axis represents the costs.

The horizontal axis represents the number of clocks sold.

Line A–B is the fixed costs of $200,000.

Line C–D is the total sales at $10.00 per clock.

Line A–E is the total costs at $5.00 per clock plus the fixed costs.

The break-even point is the sale of 40,000 clocks. At this point sales of $400,000 are equal to fixed costs of $200,000 plus the cost of 40,000 clocks at $5.00 each. The difference between lines C–D and A–E is the profit or loss.

Summary

Today we have:

● Shown why the profit and loss budget is so important and why it is often the most studied of the budgets and forecasts.

● Seen where the figures that go into this budget come from and noted that it is a summary of all the income and expenditure.

● Looked at the format of a profit and loss budget, and studied the different requirements for a trading business and a manufacturing business. We have seen that a small number of items may go straight into this budget without appearing in any other budget apart from the budgeted balance sheet.

● Seen how taxation is always a factor, though it may go into only the budgeted balance sheet.

● Had a brief look at the break-even point and break-even charts.

You probably know the importance of cash to a business and how serious it can be to run short. A good cash budget and good regular cash forecasts should make this much less likely to happen. This is the subject of our work tomorrow and at the end you will have the opportunity to prepare a cash budget.

SUNDAY

MONDAY

TUESDAY

WEDNESDAY

THURSDAY

FRIDAY

SATURDAY

Fact-check (answers at the back)

1. What is often considered to be the most frequently asked question about budgets?
   a) Why is it late? ❑
   b) Who is going to be sacked? ❑
   c) What's the profit going to be? ❑
   d) Can we afford a dividend? ❑

2. Which of the following statements is true?
   a) The profit and loss budget is a summary of assets and liabilities ❑
   b) The profit and loss budget is a summary of budgeted income and expense ❑
   c) If you get the revenue right, the rest of the profit and loss budget virtually does itself ❑
   d) The layout of the profit and loss budget differs according to whether there is a profit or a loss ❑

3. Are detailed budgets normally published?
   a) Yes, always ❑
   b) Yes, usually ❑
   c) Not usually ❑
   d) Only if the tax authorities insist ❑

4. What is turnover?
   a) Orders taken ❑
   b) Invoiced sales ❑
   c) Revenue carried forward from the previous period ❑
   d) Cancelled orders ❑

5. Can the budgeted sales figure include VAT or sales tax?
   a) Yes – but only if the tax element is then deducted ❑
   b) Yes – and it is not adjusted ❑
   c) No, never ❑
   d) No, unless special permission has been given ❑

6. Only one product is sold and the selling price is always 50 per cent higher than the price paid. Purchases are:

   January £1,000,000
   February £400,000
   March £300,000

   Invoiced sales in March are budgeted to be £1,200,000. What should be the budgeted cost of sales for March?
   a) £300,000 ❑
   b) £700,000 ❑
   c) £800,000 ❑
   d) £1,200,000 ❑

7. Which of the following is likely to be a fixed cost?
   a) Bank interest ❑
   b) Insurance premiums ❑
   c) Direct wages ❑
   d) Factory rent ❑

8. Fixed costs are $1,000,000. Each unit sold is sold for $600 and the variable cost for each unit sold is $400. What is the break-even point?
   a) $3,000,000 ❑
   b) $2,000,000 ❑
   c) $2,500,000 ❑
   d) $4,000,000 ❑

9. Which of the following often goes straight into the profit and loss budget instead of another budget?
   a) Depreciation ❏
   b) Audit fee ❏
   c) Directors' salaries ❏
   d) Investment income ❏

10. What is represented by the bottom line in a profit and loss budget?
    a) Total costs ❏
    b) Net profit or loss ❏
    c) Gross profit or loss ❏
    d) Indirect costs ❏

SUNDAY

MONDAY

TUESDAY

WEDNESDAY

THURSDAY

FRIDAY

SATURDAY

FRIDAY

The cash budget

The importance of the cash budget is often underestimated and it is certainly worth a detailed study. Today we do just that and then you will have a chance to prepare one from information provided. The cash budget should be one of the last to be prepared because many of its figures are taken or adapted from the contents of other budgets.

At the end of today's work we will have studied the main budgets usually encountered. This is with the exception of the budgeted balance sheet, which comes last of all. This is important but it will almost certainly be prepared by the accountants and is beyond the terms of this book.

The topics covered today comprise:

- Definition of cash
- The importance of the cash budget and the cash forecast
- The distinctions between cash, profit and net worth
- The preparation of a cash budget
- Cash budget exercise

Definition of cash

It is tempting, but of course very wrong, to say that cash is the notes and coins found in the petty cash box. This is part of cash, but only a very small part. Cash is the total of all the bank balances plus any notes and coins. The bank balances almost always make up virtually all the cash total. Bank borrowing must be deducted. It is possible, and indeed very common, for total cash to be a minus figure as in the following (brackets are conventionally used to indicate a negative amount):

	£
Bank balances in credit	1,000
Notes and coins	500
	1,500
Less bank overdrafts	200,000
Total cash	(198,500)

The importance of the cash budget and the cash forecast

You will probably not be surprised to be told that the cash budget and the cash forecast are extremely important. A business should aim to have the right amount of cash, not too much and not too little. Both are wrong, but not having enough is potentially much worse. Before we consider this, we will say why it is a mistake to have too much. It is because, like having too much stock, it is wasteful. Cash is tied up that could profitably be invested elsewhere or returned to the owners of the business.

Having too little cash is likely to mean that the business cannot achieve its potential. Profitable opportunities may have to be turned down. Worse, if the cash shortage is severe and unless an alternative source of finance can be obtained, the very existence of the business may be threatened. Businesses do not fold because of a lack of profits, though this of course is very unhelpful and in the long run may be fatal. Businesses fold because they cannot pay their debts as they become due. It is not uncommon for a business to fail that is making profits at the time of its failure. This is particularly true of expanding businesses.

A good cash budget and good, regular cash forecasts enable managers to manage the cash and, if problems are predicted, to take appropriate action in good time. A further reason for preparing a cash budget is that it is an essential step in preparing the budgeted balance sheet.

The distinctions between cash, profit and net worth

Cash, profit and net worth are completely different things and should not be confused, though they sometimes are, especially cash and profit. Profit is the difference between income and expenses, but not necessarily received or paid in cash. Net worth is the book value of a business as shown in a balance sheet. If the business is a company, net worth is the same as shareholders' funds. The reasons for the short-term differences between cash and profit include the following.

Timing differences

Sales are usually credited to the profit and loss account when goods are delivered or services performed. Payment is usually received from customers later. Purchases are usually debited to the profit and loss account as they are made. Suppliers are usually paid later.

Fixed assets and depreciation

Cash leaves the business when fixed assets are purchased, but in the very short term there is no effect on the profit and loss account. Depreciation is a later non-cash charge to the profit and loss account.

Loans to or from the business (including bank loans)

These affect cash but not profit, though there will very probably be an interest effect.

The purchase of investments, etc.

This affects cash but not profits.

Bad debt reserve, etc.

The creation of a reserve such as a bad debt reserve reduces profit but not cash. The later release of an over-provision increases profit but not cash.

Payment of dividends

The payment of dividends passes cash to the owners of a company. Dividends take cash out of a company and are paid out of reserves.

Taxation

Income tax and National Insurance contributions (in the UK) are payable to HMRC after they have been deducted from employees' wages and after they have affected the profit and loss account. Corporation tax (in the UK) is usually paid to HMRC after the period of the profit and loss account.

The preparation of a cash budget

The steps in doing this are as follows:

1 An appropriate form must be designed, with care being taken to ensure that the headings cover all the sources of cash coming in and all the sources of cash going out. Many different layouts are possible and a good one is shown at the end of this section of the chapter.
2 The calculated or forecast cash total at the beginning of the period covered should be entered. If it is a negative figure, which means overall net borrowing, this should be indicated in some way. It is usual to do this with brackets or a minus sign, and this also applies to negative figures throughout the document.
3 Relevant figures and totals from other budgets should be entered. In doing this, two types of adjustment are necessary:
   a) Adjustments for non-cash items should be made. For example, the following are non-cash items that may be included in the expenses and must be added back:
      – creation of a bad debt reserve
      – depreciation of fixed assets.
   b) The figures must be adjusted for timing differences. For example, it is usually necessary to do this for the following:
      – Customers will normally pay after the sales have been recorded in the profit and loss budget.
      – Suppliers will normally be paid after the purchases have been entered into the profit and loss budget or capital expenditure budget.

- Tax is normally paid to the tax authority after it has taken effect in the profit and loss budget.
4 Entries should be made for items that do not appear in the profit and loss or capital expenditure budgets. Possible examples include:
    - purchase and sale of investments
    - dividends paid.
5 The columns should be totalled and the running cash balance calculated.

Do not overlook the possibility that a cash requirement may peak between two budgeted points. It is possible for $1,000,000 to be needed on both 31 May and 30 June, but the cash requirement to be $1,100,000 on 15 June.

At this point please think about a temptation which should be resisted. What will you do if the cash budget indicates an unacceptably high or even critically high cash requirement? You might consider 'solving' the difficulty by assuming that customers will pay more quickly and suppliers will be paid more slowly. The problem is that they very understandably might not be willing to co-operate in this way. Such assumptions should be made only if it is reasonable to do so.

The following is an example of a cash budget illustrating the principles described.

Cash budget for six months to 30 June

	Jan £000	Feb £000	March £000	April £000	May £000	June £000
Receipts						
UK customers	400	400	450	450	450	500
Export customers	600	120	380	60	120	120
Government grants	10			3		
All other	4	4	4	4	4	4
	1,014	524	834	517	574	624
Payments						
Suppliers	802	407	631	506	488	482
Salaries (net)	55	55	55	59	59	59

(*continued*)

PAYE and national insurance	18	18	18	18	20	20
Corporation tax			100			
Dividends					50	
Capital expenditure	10	10	10	75	75	10
All other	10	10	10	10	10	10
	895	500	824	668	702	581
Excess of receipts over payments	119	24	10	(151)	(128)	43
Add opening bank balance	(2,016)	(1,897)	(1,873)	(1,863)	(2,014)	(2,142)
Closing bank balance	(1,897)	(1,873)	(1,863)	(2,014)	(2,142)	(2,099)

Cash budget exercise

Hopefully this is all clear and you will now be able to complete a cash budget. The form is the same but the figures are different. A few figures have been filled in to help you. Please do the rest using the following data. The answer is at the end of the chapter.

Receipts from customers

Customers are expected to pay in an average of 60 days. Budgeted invoicing is as follows:

	UK £000	Export £000
November	905	200
December	900	200
January	905	300
February	920	300
March	920	300
April	950	350
May	950	350
June	950	350

Payments to suppliers

It is expected that suppliers will be paid in an average of 30 days. Budgeted invoices from suppliers are budgeted to be as follows:

	£000
November	820
December	810
January	800
February	850
March	900
April	900
May	900
June	950

Corporation tax

A corporation tax payment of £318,000 will be paid in May.

Dividends

A dividend of £100,000 will be paid in January.

Capital expenditure

This is budgeted to be £30,000 per month during the period of the budget.

Opening overdraft

The overdraft at 31 December is expected to be £4,320,000.

Cash budget for six months to 30th June

	Jan £000	Feb £000	March £000	April £000	May £000	June £000
Receipts						
UK customers						
Export customers						
Government grants			60			

(continued)

All other	10	10	10	10	10	10
Total						
Payments						
Suppliers						
Salaries (net)	103	104	110	110	110	110
PAYE and National Insurance	34	34	34	34	34	34
Corporation tax						
Dividends						
Capital expenditure						
All other	6	6	6	6	6	6
Total						
Excess of receipts over payments						
Add opening bank balance						
Closing bank balance						

Summary

Today we have:

● Established exactly what is meant by the term 'cash'. It is sometimes misunderstood and it cannot be properly budgeted if we are not absolutely sure what it is.

● Seen just why the cash budget and the cash forecast are so important. I really do hope that you never have to find this out the hard way. Perhaps budgets are not updated during the year, but it is a good idea to do regular cash forecasts.

● Established the differences between cash, profit and net worth. They are totally different and sometimes confused. It is possible to find this out the hard way, perhaps by trying to spend the profit when there is no money in the bank.

● Looked in detail at how a cash budget is prepared and seen an example.

Finally you will, I hope, have successfully prepared a cash budget.

We have now finished reviewing the budgets, which leaves what happens afterwards. Tomorrow we will end the week by looking at how budgets and forecasts should be used after completion and approval, and at periodic statements comparing actual performance with the budget or forecast.

SUNDAY

MONDAY

TUESDAY

WEDNESDAY

THURSDAY

FRIDAY

SATURDAY

Answer to cash budget for six months to 30 June

	Jan £000	Feb £000	March £000	April £000	May £000	June £000
Receipts						
UK customers	905	900	905	920	920	950
Export customers	200	200	300	300	300	350
Government grants			60			
All other	10	10	10	10	10	10
	1,115	1,110	1,275	1,230	1,230	1,310
Payments						
Suppliers	810	800	850	900	900	900
Salaries (net)	103	104	110	110	110	110
PAYE and National Insurance	34	34	34	34	34	34
Corporation tax					318	
Dividends	100					
Capital expenditure	30	30	30	30	30	30
All other	6	6	6	6	6	6
	1,083	974	1,030	1,080	1,398	1,080
Excess of receipts over payments	32	136	245	150	(168)	230
Add opening bank balance	(4,320)	(4,288)	(4,152)	(3,907)	(3,757)	(3,925)
Closing bank balance	(4,288)	(4,152)	(3,907)	(3,757)	(3,925)	(3,695)

Fact-check (answers at the back)

1. At what stage should the cash budget be prepared?
   - a) Normally first ☐
   - b) Normally last ☐
   - c) Normally somewhere in the middle ☐
   - d) It does not matter ☐

2. Who will normally prepare the budgeted balance sheet?
   - a) The auditor ☐
   - b) Any manager who has the time ☐
   - c) The accountants ☐
   - d) The managing director ☐

3. Does bank borrowing come within the definition of 'cash'?
   - a) Yes ☐
   - b) No ☐
   - c) It depends when the borrowing is repayable ☐
   - d) Yes in internal accounts, but not in published accounts ☐

4. Is it possible to have too much cash?
   - a) No, of course not ☐
   - b) No – and if it's a problem, it's a problem that I would like to have ☐
   - c) Yes ☐
   - d) It's a silly question ☐

5. In a company, what is a good description of 'net worth'?
   - a) The amount for which the company could be sold ☐
   - b) The value of the assets ☐
   - c) What the assets would fetch in a forced sale ☐
   - d) Shareholders' funds ☐

6. A company car is purchased for $40,000 and depreciated by 25 per cent in the first year. What is the effect on the cash budget in the first year?
   - a) $40,000 ☐
   - b) $30,000 ☐
   - c) $10,000 ☐
   - d) There is no effect ☐

7. Which budget or budgets are affected by the planned payment of a dividend?
   - a) The profit and loss budget ☐
   - b) The cash budget ☐
   - c) The budgeted balance sheet ☐
   - d) The cash budget and the budgeted balance sheet ☐

8. Payment terms for a very large customer are '30 days' but they usually pay 45 days late. When should a very large invoice dated 26 January be reflected in the cash budget?
   - a) February ☐
   - b) April ☐
   - c) May ☐
   - d) Half in April and half in May ☐

9. Which of the following should be applied to the total of the expenses in the budgeted profit and loss account when calculating the cash budget?
   - a) The creation of a bad debt reserve ☐
   - b) The depreciation charge ☐
   - c) The creation of a reserve for the settlement of a pending legal claim ☐
   - d) All of the above ☐

10. What should you **not** do if the cash budget indicates a dangerously high level of borrowing?

a) Assume (without evidence) that the customers will pay more quickly ☐

b) Discuss the problem with the bank ☐

c) Sell some investments ☐

d) Organize a new issue of shares ☐

SUNDAY

MONDAY

TUESDAY

WEDNESDAY

THURSDAY

FRIDAY

SATURDAY

SATURDAY

Monitoring progress against budgets and forecasts

After the budget or forecast has been approved comes ... possibly not much or even nothing at all. This would be unfortunate but it would not mean that the budgeting or forecasting exercise had been a complete waste of time. Those involved in the preparations will have thought logically about the organization, its finances and its future. Some at least of this will remain lodged in their minds and influence their future actions. Nevertheless, failure to monitor progress would be a great pity.

What should happen, and what usually does happen, is that regular reports giving details of budgeted and actual figures are produced. These are studied by the managers and may be reviewed at a meeting. These reports and possible meetings are important parts of this chapter. The chapter ends with some important and thought-provoking points on the need to align power and responsibility.

The topics covered today comprise:

- The format of the performance reports
- Variance analysis
- Meetings to review the performance reports
- And finally ... some thoughts on power and responsibility

The format of the performance reports

Regular performance reports should be issued by the accountants. These should be in the same format as the budgets and should give the figures for the actual results alongside the equivalent budget figures. Variances should also be given and it is usual to give the figures for the period (perhaps a month) and for the year to date as well. It is not normal to give all the reports to all the managers. Instead, distribution is usually done on a pyramid basis. The senior managers get most or all of the reports – perhaps in summarized form. The more junior managers get the reports for the departments that they manage. It sounds rigid and likely to offend the more junior managers, so perhaps some sensitivity on the point would not come amiss. The following are good examples of budget variance reports. The first is for one of the departments that make up the expenditure budget and it is followed by the profit and loss budget of one of a company's divisions. This latter one is based on the figures used in Thursday's example.

	June month			June YTD		
	Budget $	Actual $	Variance $	Budget $	Actual $	Variance $
Salaries	20,000	20,006	(6)	120,000	120,400	(400)
Commission	2,000	2,600	(600)	12,000	14,000	(2,000)
Pension costs	2,000	2,000	–	12,000	12,000	–
Car expenses	6,000	5,700	300	36,000	34,200	1,800
Other travel	1,000	900	100	6,000	5,100	900
Hotel expenses	3,000	3,250	(250)	18,000	21,700	(3,700)
Meals	1,000	995	5	6,000	5,870	130
Other expenses	1,000	1,400	(400)	6,000	6,100	(100)
Postage	200	190	10	1,200	1,160	40
Stationery	200	205	(5)	1,200	1,270	(70)
Telephone	2,000	2,150	(150)	12,000	11,900	100
Miscellaneous	1,000	930	70	6,000	5,200	800
	39,400	40,326	(926)	236,400	238,900	(2,500)

	Quarter to 30 June			6 months to 30 June		
	Budget $	Actual $	Variance $	Budget $	Actual $	Variance $
Sales	1,800,000	1,809,321	9,321	3,542,000	3,627,172	85,172
Less Direct costs	936,000	961,278	(25,278)	1,789,000	1,863,222	(74,222)
	864,000	848,043	(15,957)	1,753,000	1,763,950	10,950
Directors	115,000	117,200	(2,200)	230,000	234,874	(4,874)
Sales and Marketing Department	193,000	191,662	1,338	385,000	384,119	881
Finance Department	98,000	107,311	(9,311)	196,000	212,843	(16,843)
Personnel Department	65,000	61,244	3,756	130,000	129,600	400
Administration Department	68,000	71,999	(3,999)	141,000	146,278	(5,278)
Total other costs	539,000	549,416	(10,416)	1,082,000	1,107,714	(25,714)
Net profit	325,000	298,627	(26,373)	671,000	656,236	(14,764)

In these examples the variances are expressed in monetary terms, but it is sometimes done in percentages instead of money or as well as money. If it is done in percentages, you should consider the size of the figures. An overrun of $50 on a budget of $100 is a 50 per cent adverse variance. This is a pity but in view of the small base figure it is probably insignificant. On the other hand an overrun of $50 on a budget of $10,000 is just a 0.5 per cent adverse variance.

Budget variance reports need interpreting and an initial reaction may be wrong. For example, in the variance report for the department there is a significant adverse variance for commission. A knee-jerk reaction might be to say that this is bad, but in fact it is probably very good. Businesses want sales staff to make high levels of sales and better than budgeted sales are likely to result in higher than budgeted commission. So well done the sales staff – please keep up the good work.

There are no absolute rules for the format of budget variance reports, so you should have one that suits your needs. However, there is a lot to be said for keeping it simple. Your computer system is probably capable of providing reams of analysis and some people might want you to have it, but if it is not going to be used it is of no use. In fact it is worse than that because it will take up managers' time and camouflage the information that is useful and should be used.

Variance analysis

Fairly obviously, a variance is the difference between a budgeted figure and the corresponding actual figure. Again fairly obviously, a variance can be favourable or unfavourable. The point of analysing variances is to see why the actual performance differs from the budgeted performance. With this knowledge we can use the information and understanding to try and improve unfavourable performances in the future, and to try to consolidate favourable variances so that they continue.

A variance may be measured on a very large unit, such as a whole division within a company, or even a whole company within a group of companies. It may be a complete department, such as the $16,843 unfavourable six month variance in the Finance Department in the profit and loss example in this chapter. Breaking it down further it may be a category of expense within a department. The unfavourable variance of $3,700 for hotel expenses in the expenditure budget in this chapter is an example. Why did this happen? Perhaps more nights were spent in hotels or perhaps more expensive hotels were used. Perhaps it was a combination of the two. There is often more than one factor contributing to a variance.

This last point is well illustrated by a close look at sales variances. An overall variance may be caused by three factors:

- **Price variance.** This happens because the actual sales price differs from the budgeted sales price. The price variance is (actual price less budgeted price) × actual volume.
- **Volume variance.** This happens because the actual sales volume differs from the budgeted sales volume. The volume variance is (actual volume less budgeted volume) × budgeted price.
- **Mix variance.** This happens because the proportions of different products sold (at different prices) differs from the budgeted proportions. The mix variance is the difference between the total variance and the sum of the other two variances.

This is probably quite a bit to take in and understand, but the following practical example should help.

	Budget	Actual
Product A units sold	50,000	45,000
Product B units sold	30,000	37,000
	80,000	82,000
Product A sale price	£60	£63
Product B sale price	£40	£28
Product A sales	£3,000,000	£2,835,000
Product B sales	£1,200,000	£1,036,000
	£4,200,000	£3,871,000

Total variance	£4,200,000 – £3,871,000 = £329,000	unfavourable
Price variance	(£63 – £60) × 45,000 = £135,000	favourable
	(£40 – £28) × 30,000 = £360,000	unfavourable
	£225,000	unfavourable
Volume variance	(50,000 – 45,000) × £60 = £300,000	unfavourable
	(37,000 – 30,000) × £40 = £280,000	favourable
	£20,000	unfavourable
Mix variance	£329,000 – £225,000 – £20,000 = £84,000	unfavourable

Meetings to review the performance reports

Managers should regularly receive variance reports relevant to their area of responsibility. They should review them themselves and informally discuss them with their staff, their managers and other managers whose operations may influence their performance. In addition they should probably review them with their managers and colleagues at budget review meetings.

This suggestion may well induce groans from readers whose experience of meetings is that they are frequently an expensive waste of time. Yes, they often are, but they do not have to be and sometimes they get brilliant results. This is most likely if the meetings are:

- Relatively short
- With an agenda

- Well prepared
- With the right people there
- Effectively chaired
- Designed to end with a firm understanding about what will be done and who will do it.

It can be done and I speak from experience. More years ago than I care to remember, I regularly attended monthly meetings at Ford Motor Company's Thames Foundry in Dagenham, UK. The meetings were organized along the lines described above. The plant manager was able to run a friendly, informal and very effective meeting to pick over the budget variance reports and organize corrective action where necessary. One of my colleagues had a remarkable talent as a cartoonist and he always enlivened the cover of the pack of budget variance reports with an amusing and topical offering. After all these years, thank you, Dennis. You always got the meeting off to a good start.

And finally ... some thoughts on power and responsibility

'Power without responsibility has been the privilege of the harlot throughout the ages'. These words were spoken by the British Prime Minister Stanley Baldwin in a speech in 1931 and he was referring to Lord Beaverbrook's newspapers. He had a good point and it is certainly a memorable phrase, but in the context of budgets and forecasts it is the reverse that can be cause for concern. Responsibility without power is common. To some extent this may be inevitable, but it can be unfair and demotivating. It should be avoided where possible.

It is not realistic to expect that all the costs in managers' budgets will be entirely within their control. To take just one obvious example, salary costs will be very heavily influenced by company policy. It will probably not be possible (or desirable) to manage salaries without regard to company-wide policy, though of course company-wide policy (as far as it is known) should be reflected in the budget. Nevertheless, as far as is reasonably possible, power and responsibility should go hand in hand.

It is quite common for head office costs to be allocated to divisions or subsidiary companies, perhaps pro-rata to turnover or in some other 'fair' way. So, if it is done in this way, when a division contributes 20 per cent of turnover and head office costs are £1,000,000, the division would have to absorb costs of £200,000 into its profit and loss budget. This could be said to be right because the division receives the benefits provided by head office, perhaps including such things as the personnel department and the legal department. So the divisional profit, if there is one, would be overstated if this were not done. The problem is that divisional managers whose budget and performance are affected probably have little if any control over these head office costs. The situation is one of responsibility without power.

One solution is not to allocate head office costs in this way, but to keep all of them in an overall company-wide profit and loss budget. In a very simplified form this might look like the following:

	£
Contribution of Division 1	2,820,000
Contribution of Division 2	1,341,000
Contribution of Division 3	372,000
	4,533,000
Less Head Office costs	629,000
Overall budgeted profit before tax	3,904,000

This will overcome the problem of responsibility without power, but on no account should it be overlooked that head office costs are real and, to some extent at least, incurred for the benefit of the divisions.

Another solution is to allocate head office costs to the divisions or subsidiary companies, but to do so as the deduction of a single total below the profit or loss of the division or subsidiary. This mitigates responsibility without power, but still shows the divisions or subsidiaries that costs have been incurred for their benefit. As you perhaps know, divisional managers may still feel that head office costs are too high (why do they need all those pot plants?) and have been allocated between the divisions in an unfair way. The bottom part of a division's or subsidiary's budget might look like this:

	£
Divisional loss before head office costs	314,000
Add allocated part of head office costs	220,000
Divisional loss after allocated part of head office costs	534,000

Summary

Today we have seen why it is important to monitor progress after the approval of budgets and forecasts. This process starts with the issue of the performance reports, and we have looked at two typical examples. We have also briefly reviewed meetings to monitor the progress. This should enable managers to:

- See the comparative figures.
- Work out the reasons for shortfalls and consider what might be done to put matters right.
- See what went right and consider how the satisfactory performance can be maintained.

We have looked at variance analysis, part of which, with break-even charts, is possibly the most advanced part of this book. So congratulations if you mastered it. Finally we considered the importance of, where possible, power and responsibility going together.

The section about power and responsibility is not only the last point in the chapter; it is the last point in the book. It is of general application and an appropriate place to finish.

SUNDAY

MONDAY

TUESDAY

WEDNESDAY

THURSDAY

FRIDAY

SATURDAY

Fact-check (answers at the back)

1. What should happen after the budget has been agreed?
   a) Regular reports giving budgeted and actual figures are produced ❏
   b) Nothing ❏
   c) A small budget cut should be implemented ❏
   d) Budgeted expenditure should immediately be committed ❏

2. Who should normally issue the budget variance reports?
   a) The managing director ❏
   b) The internal auditor ❏
   c) The accountants ❏
   d) The company secretary ❏

3. Variance reports should usually give the figures for the period and...?
   a) The budget for the corresponding period last year ❏
   b) The actual figures for the corresponding period last year ❏
   c) The figures for the year to date ❏
   d) The budget for the whole year ❏

4. To what can a budget variance apply?
   a) A whole company or division ❏
   b) A whole department ❏
   c) A category of expenditure (such as travel) ❏
   d) All of the above ❏

5. How is the price variance calculated?
   a) (actual price less budgeted price) × actual volume ❏
   b) (budgeted price less actual price) × actual volume ❏
   c) (actual price less budgeted price) × budgeted volume ❏
   d) (budgeted price less actual price) × budgeted volume ❏

6. Why does the volume variance arise?
   a) Because the actual sales volume differs from the budgeted sales volume ❏
   b) Because the actual sales volume is greater than the budgeted sales volume ❏
   c) Because the actual sales volume is less than the budgeted sales volume ❏
   d) Because the actual sales volume is less than last year's actual sales volume ❏

7. Budgeted sale price is £10. Actual sale price is £13. Number sold is 32,000. What is the price variance?
   a) £3 favourable ❏
   b) £3 unfavourable ❏
   c) £96,000 favourable ❏
   d) £32,000 favourable ❏

8. Budgeted volume sold is 600. Actual volume sold is 560. The budgeted price is £1,000. What is the volume variance?
   a) £40,000 favourable ❏
   b) £40,000 unfavourable ❏
   c) £600,000 ❏
   d) £560,000 ❏

9. Is it realistic to expect that all the costs in managers' budgets will be entirely within their control?
a) Yes, of course ❑
b) No, of course not ❑
c) No, but they should be as far as is reasonably possible ❑
d) No, unless it is a finance company ❑

10. Which of the following should be avoided if possible?
a) Responsibility without power ❑
b) Power without responsibility ❑
c) Both of the above ❑
d) Neither of the above ❑

SUNDAY

MONDAY

TUESDAY

WEDNESDAY

THURSDAY

FRIDAY

SATURDAY

Surviving in tough times

Good budgeting and forecasting are useful management tools and they are always important, but in tough times their importance takes on an extra dimension. As it says in Sunday's chapter, *to fail to plan is to plan to fail*. Failure is always a bad idea, but in tough times the safety margin may well be much smaller and a failure can all too easily turn into a disaster. Effective budgeting and forecasting will help plan for this not to happen and it should give early warning of impending difficulties and disasters. Information will be at hand so that avoiding action can be taken. Here are 10 crucial tips.

1 Keep the budgets and forecasts up to date

You may be familiar with the saying that yesterday's newspaper is only good for wrapping the fish and chips. Not many people are interested in old news. It can be the same for budgets and forecasts. A typical budget covers a period of a year and a great deal can happen in that time. In tough times it is more likely that the underpinning assumptions will become out of date and perhaps seriously wrong. So keep looking at the budgets and forecasts, and bring them up to date as necessary.

2 Face facts

Ostriches are popularly supposed to deal with danger by putting their heads in the sand so that they cannot be seen, but ostriches are silly birds and this tactic will not help them. It will not help you either. Look at what the budgets and forecasts are telling you and, provided of course that they are well prepared and believable, accept their messages and respond accordingly. Optimism is usually to be welcomed, but it must be tempered with realism.

3 Respond quickly

You should actively use the budgets and forecasts to plan what you are going to do, and in tough times it is particularly important that your response is made quickly. If things are going wrong, a quick and decisive response may well be rewarded and delay may well be punished. You should look at the figures as soon as they become available, decide what needs to be done and then do it as soon as possible.

4 Do not underestimate the importance of cash and the cash forecast

The cash budget, the cash forecast and the importance of cash were explained on Friday. It is possible and common to be both profitable and short of cash, a point which is frequently misunderstood, sometimes with disastrous consequences. Businesses do not fold because they are not making profits, though this is obviously very unhelpful and may be fatal in the long run. They fail because they cannot pay their bills as they fall due. The cash budget and cash forecasts are vital. In tough times cash forecasts should be done frequently, perhaps even weekly. They should be produced quickly and studied carefully, so that difficulties can be foreseen and corrective action planned.

5 Make sure that your customers pay you on time

Your cash budget and your cash forecast should tell you how badly your business needs cash. If it needs cash badly, and to a lesser extent even if it does not, it is important that your customers pay you on time. It may be tempting to 'solve' the problem by assuming that customers will pay more quickly, but unless there are grounds for this belief the temptation should be resisted. Positive action should be taken to try and make the customers honour their obligations and pay within the contractual terms. Steps may include telephone calls, letters and emails, personal visits, third-party debt collectors and ultimately legal action.

6 Changes to the capital expenditure budget might help solve cash problems

Some at least of the capital expenditure is probably discretionary. It might not need to happen at all or it might be deferred until a later date. This would take some capital expenditure out of the budget or put it back to a later period. This would, in the short term at least, reduce the need for cash. Of course such steps would have consequences because the capital expenditure was probably in the budget for good reasons. Nevertheless, it could be considered. Alternatives could be to lease the capital items or buy them on hire purchase. This way the benefits of the assets would be obtained, but the cash effect would be deferred.

7 Consider zero-based budgets

Zero-based budgets were reviewed on Monday. A feature of them is that everything must be examined and justified. This contrasts with incremental budgets, in which past figures are taken as the basis. In tough times all expenditure must be justified or jettisoned, and this is exactly what zero-based budgets do. They do have disadvantages as well as advantages and these were reviewed on Monday. One of the disadvantages is the extra time needed for their preparation.

8 Go for 'tough but achievable'

How hard should it be to achieve the budget targets? In Sunday's chapter we reviewed the various possibilities and the arguments for and against each one. There is no point in making the budget targets virtually impossible. They will not be achieved and everyone will be demotivated. There is also no point in making the targets too easy. They will be achieved, but so what? Remember the words of the Red Queen in *Alice in Wonderland*: 'All have won and all shall have prizes'. The right approach, especially in tough times, is 'tough but achievable'. Everyone should strive to reach attainable targets.

9 Do not leave everything to the accountants

If the budgets and forecasts are left to the accountants, you will probably get an elegant set of documents, but they are likely to be much more useful if a range of managers have been involved. When times are tough, you need all the managers on board. Their input is likely to contribute to more realistic budgets and forecasts, and this is exactly what you want. Furthermore, they are more likely to feel a personal commitment to seeing that they are achieved. This too is exactly what you want.

10 Keep it simple

Most of the value of budgets and forecasts can be obtained from straightforward documents, so this is what you should produce and use. Circumstances alter cases and there may be times when much more is required, but you should probably resist being deluged with information that you neither want nor need.

Answers

Sunday: 1a; 2b; 3c; 4d; 5d; 6c; 7c; 8a; 9d; 10c.

Monday: 1d; 2b; 3d; 4a; 5b; 6b; 7c; 8b; 9b; 10d.

Tuesday: 1c; 2a; 3b; 4b; 5a; 6b; 7c; 8d; 9b; 10c.

Wednesday: 1c; 2d; 3d; 4a; 5a; 6b; 7d; 8a; 9c; 10b.

Thursday: 1c; 2b; 3c; 4b; 5a; 6c; 7d; 8a; 9d; 10b.

Friday: 1b; 2c; 3a; 4c; 5d; 6d; 7d; 8b; 9d; 10a.

Saturday: 1a; 2c; 3c; 4d; 5a; 6a; 7c; 8b; 9c; 10c.